bigfoot on the brain

An Interesting Little Book About Bigfoot

Angie Williamson

BEYOND
THE FRAY PUBLISHING

ISBN 13: 979-8-89234-147-9

Cover design: Mallorie Fountain
Full Cover Design: L. Douglas Hogan

Beyond The Fray Publishing, a division of Beyond The Fray, LLC, San
Diego, CA
www.beyondthefraypublishing.com

BEYOND
THE FRAY PUBLISHING

SINCE 2019

contents

This book is dedicated to my kids, Brandi Whited and Mallorie Fountain, for participating in my Bigfoot shenanigans (sometimes against their will), but always being supportive; to my late father, Donnie Williamson, for igniting my love for tales of the unknown. My late mother, Virginia Williamson, for her prayers that are still covering me, and to them both for taking me to church and teaching me about Jesus; to my sister Karen Lee for always showing up for me; my dear friends Barb and Tom Kramer for sharing their love of Bigfoot, knowledge, talents, and time with me.

special thanks

A special thank you to my Aunt Doris and Uncle Joe Almand who were fans of my Bigfoot adventures since the beginning, and showed up when it mattered most; my Aunt Lucy (Brenda Hampson) and my 2 BFF Sherry Hendrix and Kim Murphy, for always being supportive and encouraging me in my Bigfoot adventures; Scott Deforest for the adventures, laughs, and teaching me things; Billy X for the adventures and campfire laughs; Joe X and Jonny Twobears for including me in SEB and encouraging me to step out of my comfort zone; the members of SEKRS for the friendships, teaching me things, and including me, especially Bob "Grumpy" Wilson and Darrell Neese; the crew of the Molena Bigfoot Festival for including me (Bobby Bunn and Tina Lee); my cousin Jeff Williamson; Kevin and Doris Crawford; and the other friends and family members that have been supportive and encouraged me along the way.

Tons of love for other friends and family that tolerated my unsolicited Bigfoot stories.
I know I got on y'all's nerves.

Notice: Regarding the people listed above, the inclusion of their names does not mean they agree with my beliefs and theories, nor does it mean they believe in Bigfoot. I have mentioned them based on their character and my love for them.

introduction

Well, it's 9:24 p.m. on a Wednesday night. I have never written a book before, but I feel like there's too much information/evidence out there to be ignored regarding the existence of Bigfoot. I have learned on my journey that most people really couldn't care less. Most people like to live in their bubble and inside their little box. They like to be spoon-fed by society. They will sit in their chair and consume only what's placed on their plate. Luckily, I am not that person, and I think it's safe to assume you are not that person either since you are here. Just a heads up, I write like I talk. Being a Georgia native, I have a strong Southern accent that sounds like you should be given a side of biscuits and gravy just for listening to me, so be thankful you are here to only read and not listen. Hopefully, my dialect won't be too painful for some of you. I do not claim to be a brilliant writer or storyteller, but I do have some stories to tell.

Introduction

There have been several books I have read on the topic of Bigfoot that were honestly over my head. The authors are well-educated and honestly just way smarter than me, so I often have a hard time absorbing the information. They are great books, the information is important for this field of study, and these books are very much appreciated in the Bigfoot community. I use the information often, but I must take notes and read some of the information several times, and even then, I cannot retain some of the information for long periods of time.

I decided to organize all my thoughts, experiences, credible evidence provided by others, and any information I feel is important in this little book. Trust me, there is tons more amazing information out there just waiting to be researched. This book is to help build a baseline of knowledge, whether you want to be a field researcher, or you're just a Bigfoot enthusiast. It is my desire that this book will be easy to read, easy to understand, interesting, and thought-provoking. This book is in no way intended to do anything more than provide a very basic foundation for Bigfoot research and to provide reading entertainment. I want to encourage the readers to open their own minds, and to go and seek the truth for themselves.

Everything you will read in this book are reports, situations, statements, data, etc. that have passed the test for me. If I included it in this book, then the information is truthful to the best of my knowledge. Am I someone of importance in this field of study? No, I am not. I am no more than a typical person, such as yourself, that has taken the time to do my own research. I do, however, feel strongly enough about the subject that I am led to write this book on. Can I prove Bigfoot exists? No, I cannot. If you are a die-hard non-believer looking for this book to convince you, then don't waste your time or your money here. But, if you are an open-minded, free-thinker, believer, or simply curious, then this should be an interesting book for you to read. Hopefully, you will finish this book with answers to a few of your questions, and your mind will be stimulated with even more questions. Just maybe your eyes will be opened to the realization that this world is very different from what you have been taught and conditioned to believe.

I am a Christian. I love my Savior Jesus Christ, and in a way that is probably hard for you to understand, my Bigfoot journey led me closer to the Lord due to the various materials I have studied. If you are an atheist, agnostic, or pagan, I must warn you this book will contain Christian opinions and Biblical references. I pray you still read this book, and maybe some information in this book will make you go, "hum." I have noticed that most people I have met in this field are Creationist and not Evolutionist. Most have expressed their belief in God, and many have proclaimed to be Christians. In my opinion, it is because these people are already aware of supernatural events: such as, the Resurrection of Jesus Christ, the parting of the Red Sea, the fourth man in the fire, the virgin birth of our Savior, Noah and the Great Flood, David and Goliath, the burning bush, superhuman strength, the list just goes on and on; so, an undiscovered primate in the forest wouldn't totally blow their mind. This is not to say all Christians believe in Bigfoot, because they certainly do not. Trust me, I get questioned and lectured often. Having so many people in my life that want to debate on this subject has kept me motivated in my research.

I am often reminded of a quote from author and lecturer, Wayne Dyer, "The highest form of ignorance is when you reject something you don't know anything about." This stands true when people choose to ignore Jesus Christ, and for those rejecting the whole idea that Bigfoot is real. I love it when someone cannot explain a piece of evidence they are presented with. I think it's easier for some people to not believe because they do not want "their world" disrupted. If a person doesn't believe in Bigfoot, they have nothing to really lose other than entertainment and awe. If a person doesn't believe in salvation through Jesus Christ, they have everything to lose.

how it all started

In Oct 2018, I found myself a widow. I ended up living in a camper for seven months until I was able to gather myself enough to start navigating my life again. I would go to work in the mornings, but when I came home in the evenings there would be nothing to do. A person can only watch so much Netflix, so I started watching YouTube videos. I have always loved anything regarding the paranormal. Bigfoot, Loch Ness Monster, ghost, beastly tales, etc., and I came across something about Bigfoot in Georgia. When I read there were Bigfoot sightings in Georgia, I couldn't believe it. I thought Bigfoot was just one, maybe two creatures seen a few times around Oregon or Northern California. At this point, I dove right in. I began reading everything I could find and watching every video I could find on YouTube. Thus, my journey began...

Lying in bed at night, searching for any Bigfoot videos I could find, I discovered a YouTube Channel called "Sasquatch Chronicles." I was so excited to have an actual site where I could binge Bigfoot information and reported sightings. All Bigfoot enthusiasts know about Wes Germer and his channel. I highly recommend anyone interested in Bigfoot research to start listening to podcasts. There are several really good ones now, but the ones with the eyewitness testimonies are still my favorite.

I started reading eyewitness reports and discovered the BFRO (Bigfoot Field Research Organization) and their database. I read all those reports and absorbed as much as I could, especially the reports in Georgia. There were a couple of reports close to my hometown. I was so interested in this subject, but no one really wanted to have any discussions with me about it. Most people would just laugh and tell me they couldn't believe I would even believe in such a thing. I heard the usual, "I've been in the woods my whole life...blah, blah, blah" or "Someone would have shot one by now...blah, blah, blah." I don't even have to finish typing it because I am certain you already know. You have either heard it yourself, or you have said it to a believer.

I want you to understand, I am not a person that just believes everything. I take the time to look at the evidence and listen to people, and then I make my own decisions. Have I been wrong before? Yep, sure have. Am I wrong to believe in the existence of Bigfoot now? Nope. I am not wrong at all. There is just too much evidence out there and too many eyewitness reports, plus I have seen a few things for myself. Yes, people lie, but not everyone is a liar. Indeed, there are many hoaxers and fake videos out there. Fortunately, they are usually easy to debunk. With the scientific analysis and studies done by experts such as Dr. Jeff Meldrum (Professor of Anatomy and Anthropology at Idaho State University), there are some common factors we look for in videos to help determine if it is probably a hoax, and most are fake unfortunately.

Bigfoot had become an exciting new topic for me, but of course most of my friends thought I was crazy, and very few wanted to discuss it. Then, I was having dinner one night with a new friend, and when I told him about my new hobby he did not laugh. He said, "I know they exist; I saw one." I was blown away, and I wanted to record his encounter information just so I would have it to share with others. I had read so many other reports, I took his information and tried to format it similar to other reports. This man had zero reason to lie to me, and the following is the very 1st report I completed. As you read my reports throughout this book, you will notice that my style changed. I quickly realized most people prefer reading the encounter information in story form, so that is currently my style of report. This sighting happened in my home state of Georgia.

Case File #1

Interview completed 7/28/2020

Eyewitness testimony of a 47-year-old, white-collar, professional male, resident of Newnan, Coweta County, Georgia. Eyewitness requests to remain anonymous due to the possibility of public harassment.

Incident Info and Eyewitness Testimony
Year: 1990
Location: Suches, GA (GPS coordinates: 34.6665089, -84.1263364), close to the Chattahoochee Forest National Fish Hatchery
Time of Year: Spring
Time of Day: Early evening, approximately 5:30 p.m.

Questions and Responses

What were you doing when you saw the creature? "Looking for firewood."

Were you alone? "No, it was me and three childhood friends. We all saw the creature."

Did you experience any strange feelings prior to or during the incident, such as dread,

confusion, loss of time, etc.? "We all felt the feeling we were being watched at the same time,

and then we all four saw the creature at the same time. It scared me really bad. I did not

experience any other types of feelings except my fight or flight kicked in. I do know that he knew he scared us, and I could feel he was glad he scared us."

Did you notice any type of strange smells? "No, the creature was too far away."

How far away was the creature? "About 50 yards, I guess."

How tall do you estimate the creature to have been? "About seven foot."

Did you notice any features to determine if male or female? "No."

Did you notice any facial features? "No, it was too far away. All we could really see was his

body, massive size, and the aggressive stance he took when he saw us. It was as if he bowed up

at us."

What color was the creature? "He was brown with black mixed in. He was basically like the color

of pine tree bark."

Was he standing amongst pine trees? "Honestly, I have no clue what species of trees were

around. We were just looking at the creature."

How long did you get to look at the creature? "We looked at the creature for about three minutes."

What distinguishing features did the creature have that makes you certain the creature was

not a bear? "I have seen lots of bears while growing up in the Smoky Mountains. The creature

looked at me and made eye contact."**Did the creature have shoulders?** "Yes."

Did you notice hands, feet, long arms, or any other identifying features? "No. It was later in

the day and he was standing amongst trees and underbrush. He was not standing beside a tree or

up against a tree. He was standing in visible sight, but it has been too long now for me to recall

specific details such as that."

How has the sighting affected you? "Just made me question what was really out there."

What do you think Bigfoot is? "It could be a primate that 'they, or whoever we want to call them,

don't want us to know about.' Anything outside of our comfort zone would mess people up. Does

not fit into the story—religious-biblical."

Summary of Incident

Four teen boys on spring break traveled to Suches, Georgia, for a fishing trip. The eyewitness

states no alcohol was used during the trip, and they were camping at a public campground. The

boys decided to gather firewood for an evening fire and drove down the road in search of wood

due to being in a public campground.

They were a few miles from camp and driving very slowly, looking into the wooded areas for

firewood, when all four boys spotted the creature at the same time. They easily pulled over

because they were traveling at a low speed and all exited the car to get a clearer look.

They watched the creature stand there for approximately three minutes until it took an aggressive

stance and "bowed up" at them. At that moment, they left the scene. They returned to camp and

discussed the incident all night.

The next day, they drove to the fish hatchery and told the rangers what they had witnessed. They

were advised by the employees that many strange things had been seen in the area and were told

not to "mess around" in that area again.

The eyewitness is confident in what he saw that day and is certain he was not confusing the creature with a bear.

Well, I was so proud of that report, and since I had joined a few Bigfoot groups on Facebook, I decided to post my report in a group and see what type of response I got. I was just having fun and had prepared myself to be roasted. Surprisingly, my report was welcomed by the community. One person advised me not to type in all caps because it is harder to read, and I thanked him for the advice. That one leap of faith changed my life.

I received a Facebook message from a man named Jonny Twobears. He had recently become a "knower" and was trying to form a research group in Georgia. He had read my report, and he invited me to join him, and two other men to look for evidence. He had been having a lot of Bigfoot activity close to his home, including a Class A sighting. I was so excited, but also apprehensive. Here I was plain ol' boring Angie, and I was about to meet up with some strangers in the middle of nowhere and walk around in the woods looking for Bigfoot. Was I losing my mind? I asked myself that a few times, but I knew I had to go. I remember leaving My Aunt Doris' house that morning and her questioning my decision to go. I told her then, "Doris, I can't live my whole life sitting around waiting for something to happen. I have got to go make some things happen." I meant that in a

Bigfoot on the Brain

much broader sense than Bigfoot research; however, since that time Bigfoot research has become a large part of my life.

Jonny and I stayed in touch, and it was no time before Joe X came into the picture. Joe had reached out to Jonny looking for someone to talk to. He was an Army Ranger with an impressive military career, and he had recently witnessed a Bigfoot on a military base here in Georgia. At the time Joe wanted to remain anonymous. I am sure you can understand why. Joe allowed me to type a report about his sighting, and it is as follows:

CASE FILE #3

Interview completed 9/3/2020
Eyewitness testimony of a retired military officer. Eyewitness comes from a family of military officers and was in the military for 15 years. He is an expert in the field of long-range shooting with multiple deployments. Eyewitness requested to remain anonymous due to the nature of his profession.

Incident Information and Eye-witness Testimony
Date: May 2018
Location: Military base in Georgia at a designated rifle range. Range is approximately 250 yards wide and 1000 yards long.
Time/Conditions: Mid afternoon, approximately 3 p.m., weather was clear.
Environment: Military base containing vast heavily wooded areas, a large creek, and ponds. The area is known to have a

9

large population of deer, turkey, and other wildlife due to limited hunting.

Questions and Witness' Responses

What were you doing when you had the encounter? "Military training exercises."

Did you notice any type of features to determine if male or female? No, the creature was too far away."

Did you notice any facial features? "No. What I did notice was that the creature crossed the service road in 2 steps and it had really long arms. It was walking, not running."

How far away was the creature? "About 1200-1300 yards."

How wide was the service road? "About ten feet wide."

What color was the creature? "It was a dark grayish brown. The hair looked puffy and had a shine to it."

Why do you think there have been numerous reports of sightings at military bases? "Because of the vast forest, wildlife, and very little human disturbance."

What do you think Bigfoot is? "I believe it is more of an animal because of its anti-social behaviors. Humans are naturally sociable beings, but these creatures make it a point to be anti-social." Witness goes on to state that he believes a body is needed to prove the existence of Bigfoot because no amount of photos or footprints will.

How has this encounter affected you? "I was bothered about the safety of the shooting range. I've always been open-minded to new discoveries, but when I was stationed in Washington State, I thought Bigfoot was a joke.

Summary of Incident

Witness reports he was participating in a shooting exercise at the rifle range that began about 10 am that morning. He was working with several others, including a range safety officer that would call the range hot or cold, and then account for each person there. They were shooting at steel targets varying from 300 to 950 yards out, and he was helping spot the targets by panning back and forth through his high-powered military optics. During one session, the range supervisor called the range cold so shooters could go down on the range and fix or verify their targets. He reports they drove to the targets using a golf cart, painted the targets with fresh paint, and returned to the firing line. As the range safety officer saw each shooter back into place, he made the announcement, "all ready on the firing line". The witness stated, "I got down back behind my spotting scope. I was looking down at a series of targets at the farthest end of the range and the range safety officer gave the command, 'the range is hot', and the shooters started firing. I was spotting for several shooters, so I had to pan left-to-right from time-to-time. At one point, I could see down a long service road/firebreak on the backside of the range (I had top-notch optics). I saw an individual on two legs walk across the service road from right to left in two steps. At first, I thought it was someone, but who in their right mind would be walking in the area bullets are being fired towards, and not be taking cover when they heard rifle shots? The range officer called a cease fire because he also saw something. He called Range Control and verified that we were the only 'hot' range, and no service personnel were working in the small arms impact area. There were also no trainings scheduled that day"

Additional Comments

Witness states that he was using a Leupold MK-4 spotting scope that day, and he is well-trained in identifying individuals through the scope. The witness returned at a later date and used a laser range finder in an effort to determine range and size of creature. He estimates the creature was approximately seven-foot-tall and weighed a minimum of 300 pounds.

The witness reports that during a Super Challenge Competition in January that following year, two service men on duty reported seeing a "very tall person in a ghillie suit crossing the road" about ¾ mile away from his sighting. He reports that all competitors were accounted for, and there is no explanation for an individual to do that on a military base, especially after dark.

By the time of this report, I had already completed my 2nd report from a man that lived in New York. I was beginning to learn that for every twenty that scoff at the idea, there's one sitting quietly wanting to talk to someone about what they experienced. Many also want to share the story of a family member or close friend. This report, "Case File #2", is included in Chapter 8 and is a two-part report.

After some time passed, Jonny and Joe contacted me about starting a YouTube channel and podcast. I accepted the challenge because why not? I was becoming this person that had never existed before, and I was really stepping out of my comfort zone. My cousin Jeff Williamson wrote music we could use, and then he worked to compile various recordings to create our introduction music. We loved it. We filmed our 1st podcast, and soon had a few others join us. Scott DeForest, Happy Harris, and Hank Rosser joined the team soon after.

Jonny, Joe, and Scott were on a research project not long after the group formed, when they all

witnessed a juvenile bigfoot and an adult on the same day. One even "spider crawled". This is their story to tell, so I recommend you check out the podcast about what happened at "The Happy Place." Here is the link to the first episode of this being discussed. There are several more videos on the podcast where this is discussed with other pieces of evidence also.

https://www.youtube.com/live/NU4vM90u2gE?si=
we_D3UDu-FdSdBB0

If you cannot access this link, you can search YouTube, "The Sasquatch Encounter Brigade." You will be able to find the videos there.

I decided I was going to start going out into the field too. "Squatching" is all fun and games during the day, but when night falls it can become extremely scary for a sissy like me. For my first overnight research project, I met Scott Deforest and Billy X at an undisclosed location. I had never met these men in person and agreed to just meet up and stay in the woods overnight. Again, I was questioning my decision-making abilities at this point, but I am so glad I did it. I made two great friends and have learned so much since then. Scott DeForest is one heck of a teacher, and I will always be appreciative of him taking time to teach me things. There is a lot to learn when you get into the field of Bigfoot field research, things that you would never imagine. If you want to get into field research, I highly recommend you find your-self a Scott. Link up with a seasoned researcher because you will make a lot of mistakes and may miss a lot of details if you don't.

Anyway, I was terrified once darkness fell. Hearing distant howls of strange creatures and seeing weird heat signatures really messed with my head. I think I developed "Bigfoot on the Brain". I coined it that night, because I thought everything was a dang Bigfoot. I am certain I got on the guys' nerves, but we laughed so much sitting around that fire, I think they forgave me. That was truly one of the funniest and most entertaining camping trips of my life. I also need to note that I was too terrified to sleep in a tent. I slept in my truck, parked facing the exit, with the keys in the ignition. I woke up probably every 30 minutes and peeked out hoping I could see one crawling around but also hoping I didn't. I might have passed out if I had seen one that night for sure. I have been out several times now, and I am not nearly as scared as I once was. I have gotten over "Bigfoot on the Brain" I think, and I have graduated to sleeping in a tent... sometimes.

The real kicker was when Scott and I went to Ware County, Georgia on an investigation. I completed a report about that and what happened to us. You can find that report as Chapter 9, "The Okefenokee Report." That is also when I met my friends Barb and Tom Kramer. You really do meet some amazing people when you get into the world of Bigfoot.

Barb and Tom lived near the Okefenokee Swamp, and I deemed Barb my swamp expert. Any questions I had about the swamp, I would just ask Barb. Barb helped me a lot with that project, and they have both become involved in research, and helping with the Molena Bigfoot Festival in Molena, Georgia every November. Molena is in Pike County, where the Elkin's Creek casting was done, and is the most "Bigfoot Friendly" town in the south in my humble opinion. We will talk more about the Elkins Creek cast in Chapter 6.

what is bigfoot, you ask?

Well, honey I wish I knew. If anyone tries to convince you they know exactly what Bigfoot is, please take your questions to another researcher because until something is proven, everything is speculation and opinions. We all have a lot of theories and assumptions, but until we know for sure, we don't know anything. I hope one day we can determine exactly what these creatures are without requiring a body. I think you will find most of us do not want one harvested for science, but I am afraid that is what it is going to take.

Be prepared to hear all sorts of theories regarding what these creatures are. I will list the most common theories I have found, and in no specific order.

1. Nephilim or descendants of the Nephilim-the offspring of the fallen angels and human women.

Thought to possibly be the giants referred to in the Bible.

2. Relict Hominoid-An ancient primate yet to be discovered.

3. Descendants of Gigantopithecus-A giant bipedal ape that once walked the Earth before its extinction.

4. Alien-Bigfoot sightings are often reported near UFO sightings.

5. Mystical Creatures aka "The Woo" This has been a term used by those that believe Bigfoot can do things such as travel through portals, shapeshift, cloak, disappear, etc. Native Americans believe they can travel to other dimensions and possess psychic abilities. There have been many reports of strange phenomena surrounding these creatures, especially on Native American Reservations. Many strange phenomena around Bigfoot have been reported by other races, and all regions around the world.

This list can go on; chimera, demons, skinwalkers, or just plain ol' monsters from another dimension. My personal opinion, which can totally be wrong because that is all it is... an opinion, but I believe they are a type of ancient humanoid creature that has maintained supernatural abilities given to them by God at creation. I can only imagine the super abilities we as humans may have had in the beginning, before we filled our brains and our stomachs with garbage. We allow ourselves to be spoon-fed information and just accept it all as truth. We live in structured environments and have become creatures of habit. We consume the poisons we are fed, to our bodies and our minds. We get up at the same time each morning, travel the same route to work, repeat the same duties each day, go to bed at the same time each night, and drown ourselves in movies, social media, music, books, etc. These creatures are part of the earth itself. They belong to the night. Deep in the woods, under the cover of darkness is where they thrive. Can you imagine how keen their senses must be? Think of the incredible senses and talents so many animals have, combine all those senses and talents, then add a brain with the ability to think, reason, plan, and communicate. A supernatural force of nature. They remain as organic as the day God made them.

Consider all the amazing abilities some animals possess. The chameleon can vanish into his/her surroundings. Elephants, whales, giraffes and many more use infrasound to communicate and hunt. There is also the incredible night vision many animals possess to think about.

A chameleon can change its color by changing the different pigments in its skin. The first assumption would probably be that this talent is impossible for Bigfoot because of all the body hair. Well, consider the hair of the polar bear. People usually assume polar bears are white, but their hairs are translucent and hollow. This allows lights to reflect while allowing the black skin beneath to absorb heat.

Here's a thought. What if the same is true for Bigfoot? What if they can change the pigments on their skin just enough to allow them to disappear into their surroundings, just as the chameleon does? It does not require a large variation of colors to camouflage yourself into a bush. That is just a possible theory of course. Even if they cannot change the color of their skin, having hairs that can absorb and/or refract light could also play a huge part in making them appear to vanish into the forest.

Infrasound is an extremely low frequency that humans cannot hear. It allows animals to communicate over long distances and works especially well in dense forests. Although humans cannot hear infrasound, we can feel it. Tigers are known to use infrasound while hunting prey because infrasound can penetrate bones and cause tempo-rary paralysis. There have been many cases of people reporting possible infrasound hits from Bigfoot. It is not uncommon for an eyewitness to also report symptoms such as headaches, dizziness, confusion, or feelings as if their internal organs had vibrated. Would it not be so extreme to think a Bigfoot could use infrasound to confuse someone that accidentally got too close?

Regarding the incredible night vision some animals possess, the nocturnal animals have large eyes and have more rods than cones in their eyes. Rods pick up light, allowing nocturnal animals to see even when it is completely dark. Many animals also have something called a tapetum lucidum. This is the reflective layer that lies behind the retina, and it allows even small traces of light to reflect off the membrane. This is what we refer to as "eyeshine" and it gives the eye another chance to use the light. Bigfoot eyes have been reported to reflect light so vibrantly they appeared to glow. What I saw in Waycross, Ga. one night fits this description perfectly. Be sure to read "Our Story" in Chapter 9.

Consider all the things discussed in this chapter. A nocturnal creature, with abilities and talents that surpass any animal known to man. Add brute strength and cognitive abilities, and you have an Apex Predator that is at the top of its food chain. I certainly do not want to cross one in a bad mood.

three
relict hominoid

What is the difference between a Hominid, a Hominin and a Hominoid? A hominid group includes all extinct and modern Great Apes, including modern humans, whereas a hominin group only includes humans and "immediate" ancestors. The term "immediate" is used in the description of the hominin group because evolutionists believe all primates evolved from a common ancestor, but only immediate ancestors have been confirmed. The Hominoid group includes the Hominid group, but also includes the gibbons, and adds brachiation skills and higher intelligence than other primates as a characteristic. (AmazingLife.Bio, n.d.). According to Dr. Jeff Meldrum, in an interview completed by Merritt Herald YouTube, on August 14, 2024, at the Nicola Valley Bigfoot Conference, this would be the group Bigfoot would fit into.

We know God made different types of primates. We recognize five types of the Great Apes: human, orangutan, gorilla, bonobo, and chimpanzee. Chimpanzees and bonobo are the closest to humans and considered the most intelligent of all animals. In many ways we look and behave like apes. According to Morgana Diamantopoulos with the Jane Goodall Institute, there are 5 ways chimps are like humans in their behaviors.

1. Empathetic and feel a wide range of emotions and provide help to one another.
2. Respect for their elders.
3. Love to have fun and play.
4. Compassionate and sociable
5. Resourcefulness (Johnson, 2022)

It wasn't until I started studying Sasquatch that I learned of the scientific evidence that modern man (Homo sapiens) evolved in Africa, and there is not a particular Homo sapiens individual that researchers recognize as being the specimen that gave Homo sapiens its name, according to the Smithsonian. Would that be "the missing link?" Being a Christian, that just confirms creation even more to me. Science cannot identify where exactly Homo sapiens originated from, but believe we evolved from Homo heidelbergensis and co-existed with Neanderthals, Homo erectus, and Homo floresiensis, yet we are the only surviving species today.

I graduated in 1985, and I remember the chart from our textbooks showing the stages of evolution. It started with a chimpanzee, then several stages of evolution for man, a missing link, and then modern man. Now, we know there were Neanderthals, Denisovans, and possibly other early human species in addition to modern man that lived during the same time periods. Again, we know modern man began in Africa, and we know that people of European and Asian descent typically have a small percentage of Neanderthal, whereas Africans do not. We do not know what happened to the Neanderthal people, but they seemed to disappear approximately 40,000 years ago, after inhabiting Europe and Asia over 350,000 years. They may have been killed by modern man or may have simply bred out by mating with modern man. (Handwerk, 2021)

I wondered how the whole population was destroyed during the flood except for Noah's family, and only those with European and Asian ancestors carry a Neanderthal DNA. I was stumped because if we are all descendants of Noah, and the Neanderthals were before and during early modern man, then we should all have Neanderthal DNA, or no one should.

I began to study more about Neanderthals, and I came across some studies that believe they did not live as long ago as evolutionists would have us believe because DNA cannot live that long. According to BBC Science Focus, every 1,000 years, about 75% is lost in genetic information. Honestly, for every study you find that says DNA has been found dating as old as 70,000 years ago, you can find a study that argues this cannot be true. I am not qualified to make a scientific determination, but I do believe in the Great Flood.

Probably one of the best explanations you will find is one I found on "Patterns of Evidence" podcast titled, "Biblical Genetics Episode 4: Are Neanderthals Human"? Dr. Rob Carter, a Geneticist, of Creation Ministries International, and Timothy Mahoney discuss this very topic. It is Dr. Carter's belief that it stemmed from the fall of the Tower of Babel. The Tower of Babel is mentioned in the Bible. In the Book of Genesis, it describes a tower built by the people in an attempt to reach Heaven. This angered God so he confused their languages, destroyed the tower, and the people were scattered.

Dr. Carter goes on to explain that modern man has been genetically proven to come from one female and one male, for the entire human race. Since this is not a book to educate you on Neanderthals, I encourage you to investigate this subject and give this podcast a listen because the genetic information he provides is very interesting and just further solidifies Adam and Eve. You can go to creation.com to access some of Dr. Carter's videos and information on creation. *(Biblical Genetics-Patterns of Evidence Foundation (Patterns+), n.d.)*

Another possibility to consider in my own personal opinion, would be that one of Noah's daughters-in-law had Neanderthal DNA, such as Japeth's wife since it is believed that

Japath and his descendants settled Europe and Asia. If this were the case, then that would place Bigfoot on the Ark, along with all the other animals. That is, if Bigfoot is simply a primate.

Considering all the similarities, is it so far-fetched that another group of primates, yet to be discovered, could be living in clans, helping each other, hunting and gathering, utilizing resources such as the cover of darkness, cave systems, and dense forest to remain hidden all these years? Many people believe they are no more than an undiscovered primate. A type of ape that falls somewhere between a human and the other great apes. Most reports describe them as having an ape-like appearance ranging from human features to almost orangutan, and other variations in between. For Bigfoot to have remained a mystery all this time, he or she would require intelligent thinking abilities and almost supernatural survival skills. The caloric intake necessary for a creature of that size would require a lot of food, unless they possess the ability to slow down their metabolism when food is not plentiful. I want Bigfoot to be a flesh and blood creature, but I cannot say that is all he/she is. I think it is possible Bigfoot is a Relict Hominoid that has maintained abilities given to them at creation, by God Almighty. Abilities that we as humans cannot understand.

four
could they be descendants of gigantopithecus?

Gigantopithecus is believed to be a giant ape that lived across China but became extinct approximately 300,000 years ago. Once thought to be a hominin (a type of human), "it is now thought to be closely allied with orangutans." (Wikipedia) The hominin theory of these creatures lost footing because evidence of this creature has only been found in China, and Homo sapiens began in Africa. Considering there have been many reported sightings of Bigfoot resembling an orangutan, especially the skunk ape reports, it gives some credence to this theory.

There is a very well-known set of pictures in the Bigfoot community known as the "Myakka Ape" where the creature does resemble an orangutan, except it is a dark color instead of the orange orangutan color. Here is one link where you can see the pictures and read about the incident and judge

for yourself. https://youtu.be/mdez-m4bRa8?si=OzXC1xft
dEv4pnmg

One well-known researcher, the late Grover Krantz (1931-
2002), risked his career as an anthropologist to publicly
study Bigfoot. According to author Brian Regal, with The
National Library of Medicine, he attempted to prove the
creature's existence by applying to the problem the tech-
niques of physical anthropology: methodologies and theo-
retical models that were outside the experience of the
amateur enthusiasts who dominated the field of anomalous
primate studies. (2009)

It was Krantz's belief, and some of today's researchers, that
Bigfoot may be a descendant of Gigantopithecus. With
varying descriptions of how today's creatures look, ranging
from an almost human appearance to an orangutan, one
must wonder why some of the species began to look more
humanlike, whereas others have maintained such a resem-
blance to an orangutan.

Those that believe in the Gigantopithecus theory, believe
that Gigantopithecus may have migrated to North America
from Asia via the Bering Strait. Gigantopithecus fossils have
never been discovered outside of Asia, and the main evidence
that these giant apes ever existed is based solely on fossilized
teeth and jawbones discovered in caves. No skeletons have
been found, but the four partial jawbones and 2000 plus
teeth found, according to science, are considerable evidence

that these animals existed and would have stood over 10 feet tall and weighed 1,200 pounds or more.

five
nephilim, aliens, and the woo

I will attempt to summarize these theories for you. Please understand these are only theories as I understand them, and there are other variations and opinions available for your research. When I started writing this book it was my intention to discuss each of these individually in separate chapters, but with these three topics, it just became easier for me to group them together. They may or may not be connected, but it gets more confusing trying to refer to information already provided, so I decided the simple way is the best way.

It wasn't until I began researching Bigfoot that I learned about the Book of Enoch, and the "Missing Books of the Bible" known as the Apocrypha, meaning "secret" or "things hidden away." The manuscripts of some of the books were found among the Dead Sea Scrolls, leading scholars to believe these texts were once considered to be Scripture because of their preservation. Now, before you start thinking

I have been influenced into believing false teachings, let me explain a few things. First, it encouraged me to learn more about the Bible itself and its history, and secondly, some of the views and opinions discussed in this chapter do not match my own. Living in the Bible Belt all my life, it has been pounded into my head to read only the King James Translation, which I have adhered to for over 50 years, and now I learn there were books removed that were previously in the Bible for over 2000 years.

The King James Translation was completed in 1609 but was not published until 1611. An archbishop and 47 scholars/clergymen were commissioned by King James to interpret the Bible from Latin and Greek into English, and at that time the Bible contained 80 books. It contained the Old Testament, The Apocrypha, and the New Testament. At the time, the Catholic view was that 12 of these books were Canonical Scripture, and some of these are still included in the Old Testament of the Catholic Bible. Then in 1885, about 20 years after the Civil War ended, "The Apocrypha" was removed from the Protestant Bible in the U.S., leaving the current 66 books now referred to as "The Canon." There is controversy as to why the books were removed. Most Protestant Christians believe they were removed from the Bible because they were not considered as Scripture. Some also believe they contain some contradictions. (M, 2024) This is a very complex subject and can get extremely confusing, especially if you do not study and learn the history of the Bible from the very beginning. It has been a fascinating journey for me, and I highly recommend studying the creation and evolution of the Bible.

Now, after that brief Bible history lesson it is time to discuss the Book of Enoch. Genesis 6:1-4 and the Book of Enoch are the basis for the theory that bigfoot may be Nephilim. The Book of Enoch is a fascinating book providing information on the origins of demons and the Nephilim, and explanations regarding the Great Flood of Noah. The Book of Enoch was found in the Dead Sea Scrolls and was widely read between (516 BCE-70 CE), when the 2nd Temple stood in Jerusalem, and I do believe it should be considered ancient text just as the other books of the apocrypha.

Through my research and readings, I mistakenly thought The Book of Enoch was originally part of the apocrypha that was removed from the Christian Bible, when in fact it was never included in the Roman Catholic or Protestant Bible. The Book of Enoch is one of the books of the Pseude-pigrapha, meaning literature affecting the style of biblical writings and authored by a biblical character, but it only remains in the Ethiopian Bible. It is thought that it may have had a direct influence on some books of apocrypha. The Book of Enoch was not written by Enoch, but by several others throughout the centuries before Christ. According to Robert Bagley with Northern Seminary, Jesus even referred to The Book of Enoch multiple times, such as Matthew 5:5 and Luke 6:24; and his brother Jude, quoted a verse from The Book of Enoch, Jude 1:14-15. (n.d.) Apparently, Jesus and his earthly family considered the book to be worthy of reading. To be fair, there was no written language during Enoch's lifetime, therefore he would have relied upon oral records to be passed down through the generations, until they could be transcribed.

The purpose of this chapter is not to do an analysis on the Book of Enoch, but to explain to you where these theories are derived from. I am not a Biblical scholar, and I do not claim to have a full understanding of the Dead Sea Scrolls, the "Missing Books", or the "Lost Books" of the Bible. I have written all of this as it is my understanding.

The Nephilim may have been the giant beings mentioned in the Bible. According to the Book of Enoch, these giants were created when the fallen angels had children with human women, and a lot of people believe that KJV Genesis 6:1-4 confirms this theory. Those verses are read as follows:

1. "And it came to pass, when men began to multiply on the face of the earth, and daughters were born unto them."
2. "That the sons of God saw the daughters of men that they were fair; and they took them wives of all which they chose."
3. "And the Lord said, my spirit shall not always strive with man, for that he also is flesh: yet his days shall be an hundred and twenty years."
4. "There were giants in the earth in those days; and also after that, when the sons of God came in unto the daughters of men, and they bear children to

them, the same mighty men which were of old,
men of renown."

Notice in that verse where it says, "and also, after that." This is why some people believe the fallen angels continued to breed with human women for a period of time. We also know that giants continued after the flood, because the 12 spies Moses sent out reported finding giants living throughout the land of Canaan. If all flesh was destroyed in the flood except for Noah and his family, how did giants come to exist again? Could it have been that the fallen angels began to mate with human women again? The Book of Enoch also states that the fallen angels even mated with animals, and this is where some other believers theorize Bigfoot may originate from. I have to admit Bigfoot is reported to appear as a mix of great apes and humans, with amazing abilities beyond human understanding. The problem I have with this theory is that Bigfoot procreate, and no part of me believes that anything remotely connected to Satan has the ability to create life.

Some people believe Sasquatch could possibly be aliens. There are reports on sightings involving Bigfoot and UFOs, and it is uncanny how many reported sightings are in the same areas for both. Numerous eyewitness reports of tracks just stopping in the middle of a field as if the creature was just beamed up or vanished in thin air. Reports of portals, orbs, strange lights, and the strange ability Bigfoot seems to have to disappear. If Bigfoot is some type of extraterrestrial being, this could explain why a body has not been found. I mean, I believe bodies have been found and seized by the government, but I cannot prove that, so we must consider all possibilities and remain open-minded. I can't really write a lot about this theory because I simply cannot wrap my head around it. I am not saying they are wrong, but I don't have a lot of background knowledge regarding this particular theory.

Indigenous people have associated this creature with the spiritual world for hundreds of years. Again, I really want Bigfoot to be flesh and blood. I do not want to be out in the swamps looking for something that can shapeshift and God knows what else, but I cannot deny what happened on a trip to Okefenokee swamp that involved an orb. All you have to do is google "Bigfoot and Native Americans", and you will find tons of information. Every Native American tribe has a name for this elusive creature, which is where the name "Sasquatch" comes from. The name Sasquatch means "hairy man" or "wild man". In addition to the centuries of stories passed down through the generations, there are also ancient drawings of what many believe are Sasquatch on cave walls. Some Native Americans believe Sasquatch have the ability to cross in and out of the spiritual world and serve as some type of guardians. Others believe Sasquatch is a potentially dangerous entity that steals children and delivers curses.

There are currently a lot of researchers studying possible "markers". Often trees will be found in strange positions or stacked in such a way that is not natural. Could the "markers" many believe are left behind by Bigfoot represent something? Many believe they do. Structures often forming an "x", asterisks, or even pinned trees are thought to have some meanings. Could they be markers for portals, travel directions, or simply a sign for other Bigfoot to read saying, "this area is claimed by another clan?" I personally think most of that is natural fall, but I have seen a few suspicious looking markers myself. Things I can't explain, such as a whole area in the middle of a swamp where all the trees in just that one area were bent over and pinned to form arches everywhere. Every tree was pinned. Where the treetop touched the ground, another limb or limbs were placed on it to hold it down.

These are just some brief summaries to help you understand what I think are the most common theories of what Bigfoot is.

why do i believe?

Let's dive right into some reasons I believe. I am almost a knower, and maybe by the end of this book I will be able to say I am 100% a knower. The difference between a believer and a knower is that a knower has seen one and there is no denying to themselves what they saw. I had an experience near the Okefenokee Swamp in South Georgia which I will talk about a few chapters later, but right now let's discuss the reasons I am a believer.

I am going to provide you with different links and very brief descriptions, and I encourage you to click on the links if possible, and if not, then type the links into the search bar and research this evidence for yourself. There is already so much information readily available on these topics, I do not feel the need to go into deep detail about each one. If you are truly interested in the subject, then hopefully you will enjoy watching the videos and learning more about these creatures.

#1-The Patterson-Gimlin Film. If you are not familiar with that film, October 20, 1967 two men named Roger Patterson and Bob Gimlin filmed a female sasquatch in northern California. That film is probably the most controversial piece of evidence so far. Numerous studies have been made on this film clip, and everyone I have seen proves there is no way that could have been a man in a costume. Here is a link to a video by "Squatch Mafia" if you are not familiar with the video I am referring to. https://youtu.be/2Dyakc JB7Q8?si=_tnq9RAmY1LRKhWa.

#2-"Thinker Thunker"-Video analysis of The Patterson-Gimlin Film. https://youtu.be/lECNg10fJ9I?si= YxoM2MH49krG9nTT. Thinker Thunker has many incredible videos on his YouTube Channel where he provides scientific breakdowns in an effort to debunk or prove Bigfoot videos are hoax or real. There are a lot of videos on his channel that will blow your mind, and I encourage you to see for yourself. He does a phenomenal job!!!

#3-The Sierra Sounds. These are audio recordings by Al Berry and Ron Morehead, of Sasquatch vocals in the Sierra Mountains of Northern California. These recordings have been analyzed numerous times, and are proven to be out of human range. According to the experts, they are also believed to possibly have a language, which you can hear in the recordings. You can find a lot of information about these recordings online. This is one of the pieces I send to the skeptics and the non-believers that like to give me a hard time, and so far not one person can offer an explanation. Here is a link from MelBlanc222 YouTube Channel. https://youtu.be/VGfIIjN-P7o?si=AL6rFK3VnkThp0cR.

#4-The Elkin's Creek Casting. In 1993 a sheriff's deputy in Pike County, Georgia cast a footprint measuring over 17" at Elkin's Creek. Upon analysis, this casting was verified to have dermal ridges, proving this cast was of an actual barefoot and was not a hoax. The deputy, James P. Akin, went on to write a book about the incident and the cast. It is titled, *Elkins Creek*, and you can order the book online. The community of Molena, Georgia, in Pike County began holding an annual 5K and Bigfoot Festival in 2022. The race and festival are held the 2nd Saturday in November, and we have a lot of fun. I was blessed to become involved with this event in the beginning, and I enjoy watching the event grow every year. You can find the group on Facebook as "Molena Bigfoot Fest & Elkins Creek 5k + 1 Mile Fun Run/Walk. If you are interested in attending the event, send us a request to join the group to receive all the latest information. We would love to have you.

#5-Eyewitness testimonials. I realize people lie, but as I have said before, not everyone is a liar. People also make mistakes, but most people know what they see. I have read so many eyewitness accounts, and completed numerous eyewitnesses reports myself, of people that I feel were credible witnesses. I have included my reports in this book. Some of my reports will contain people I knew before I became "a squatcher", but most are from friends I met along the way. It is amazing how many people want to get these experiences off their chest and have held on to these experiences for years due to fear of ridicule or being called crazy or a liar. As I mentioned earlier in the book, Sasquatch Chronicles is the premiere eyewitness channel. If you love eyewitness testimonials as much as I do, be sure to listen. Wes Germer is the host, and here is a quick link to the YouTube Channel, but you can also find the show on almost all the streaming platforms. https://www.youtube.com/@SasquatchChronicles.

#6-My own personal experience near the Okefenokee Swamp in South Georgia. My experience involved an orb, so now I cannot deny there is some type of paranormal element to these creatures. I have included "The Okefenokee Report" in this book, which will include our story about what happened that night.

#7-Jeff Meldrum-Professor of Anatomy & Anthropology at Idaho State University. He is the author of _Sasquatch: Legend Meets Science_, and is known for his work analyzing cast, and collaborations in video analysis, laboratory research, and field research regarding Bigfoot.

The following is a link from his appearance on "The History Channel." https://youtu.be/5J4LTNb-8Hw?si=QBnc0nHoZIAJ43XQ.

#8-the 911 calls. There are actually 2 different calls. One is known as the San Antonio Call, where a homeless couple watched a Bigfoot type creature devour a deer that had been killed by a vehicle. Here is the link to a YouTube channel by The Diggem, where you can listen to the call.

https://youtu.be/Mk-XiuFNi9E?si=uGO2uf7uqT MVVh7X. The 2nd one is a call that came in from Washington State in 1990, where the man is reporting seeing the creature in his yard and tells the 911 operator his dog was also killed a few days prior. Here is a link to listen to the call on MelBlanc222 YouTube channel. https://youtu.be/ ntgR_bbpdyo?si=Wiy2v-UpKroK_IU0. I will admit, both of those recordings freak me out a little.

#9- The BFRO Database (www.bfro.net) A collection of sightings deemed credible by an organization called the Bigfoot Field Research Organization. It is a network of volunteers that collect reports from all over the United States and Canada. Be sure to check out the reports in your state. You may find one in your area.

Those are the main sources for my original belief, but since I started researching, I have been privy to a few thermal videos, trail cam pics, and some incredible testimonies from some other researchers that I have a lot of respect for. This is just one of those things where you don't realize the magnitude until you become involved. There's a lot of citizen research groups going out into the field now, and networking and sharing information. There is often information the average person will never hear about, unless they become involved in the Bigfoot subculture themselves.

I cannot talk about the Florida Skunk Apes without mentioning David Shealy and his well-known recording of a possible skunk ape on July 8, 2000, in the Florida Everglades. Here is the link to watch this video. https://youtu.be/ LmRBUSK_Dsg. I admit I was at first skeptical of this recording because of the odd behavior of the creature, but a person cannot run through the sawgrass as this beast is notably doing. While this video is not one of the original pieces of evidence that convinced me Sasquatch is real, I still consider this video to be a great piece of evidence.

I know a team of researchers that went to the location to conduct a research study and attempted to re-enact the event numerous times. The Mid Florida Bigfoot Research Team is founded by Marie Dumont, and she has become a friend and someone I highly respect. In the 25+ years since the event, no one has ever gone to the exact location to conduct any kind of research to determine whether or not it could have been a real Skunk Ape. The Mid Florida Bigfoot Research Team stepped up and took the initiative to search for the truth themselves.

During the course of their research study and multiple attempts at running the same course thru water, mud, and high sawgrass in the Big Cypress area, Marie and her team (Mike Aguilar, Chris Hensley, Ruby Jo Brew, and Kaylen Aguilar) determined the impossibility of someone in a costume having the ability to run that distance thru 1-2 feet of water as the creature did in Shealy's video in the dead heat of summer. You can access the information of the study Marie, and her team did on their website: www.midfloridabigfoot.com/david-shealy-study. Their research study video can be seen here: https://www.youtube.com/watch?v= 5PH0Im2LquM.

I also need to mention some amazing thermal footage captured by Jonny Twobears. Jonny has a lot of great videos on his YouTube Channel, The Sasquatch Encounter Brigade, but the thermal image of a possible sasquatch face watching him from the bushes is mind-blowing to me. You can see it for yourself at https://youtu.be/mOPCPJFubOk? si=r9HZSEfRW1xAij1J. His video is one of the best pieces of evidence I have ever seen. I was already a believer before he captured this footage, but this just solidified my beliefs even more.

seven
where are the bodies?

I will do my best to address these two most asked questions of all. Do you believe bears exist? How many bear carcasses have you found in the forest? How many dead bears have you seen in your lifetime that died of natural causes? I am going to make a guess and say zero, unless you spend way more time in bear country than the typical person does. Also, the bear population is much greater than the suspected Bigfoot population, so you are way more likely to find a bear than you are a Bigfoot.

When an animal dies in the forest, the forest consumes the body rather quickly. Within a few days most of the body will be consumed by scavengers, and bones will be scattered about. Some scavengers will drag parts of the animal away to consume. In the event the animal is not scavenged sooner than later, millions of maggots and other flesh-eating insects begin to consume the body. Within just a few days all that will remain are bones and fur. Even the bones will be consumed by herbivores and carnivores. Squirrels and other rodents are known to gnaw on bones, including human bones often hindering investigations of homicide victims.

Some animals also demonstrate death rituals. Elephants, crows, chimps, dolphins, and even giraffes have been known to behave in incredible ways following the death of an offspring. Some species of elephants are known to bury their deceased offspring, and as gross as it sounds, there have been reports of apes eating their dead. It is considered rare, but it does happen.

In a previous chapter we discussed the social structure found in apes that had a lot of similarities with humans, and chimps especially appear to mourn their dead. Some mothers will carry the body of a dead infant for months, whereas other times they seem to spend time with the body and seem to watch over the body for an extended period of time if a troop member dies.

Considering we believe Bigfoot lives in clans and family units, it is probably safe to assume there are strong social bonds among them. These creatures typically move under the cover of darkness, and it is believed they may utilize cave systems for shelter and travel. We believe they use creeks, rivers, railroad tracks, and power lines as a means of navigation and travel but tend to stay deep in the forest as far away from civilization as possible except on rare occasions.

At this point it is pretty obvious they know their safety depends on staying as hidden from man as possible.

Now, let's talk about trail camera pictures. We have already determined that Bigfoot are more than likely nocturnal, which means their sense of smell is already greater than the creatures of the day. We know that bears can smell trail cameras for a number of reasons, so who is to say that Bigfoot can't also smell them. One reason is human smell, but many theorize bears can smell the batteries in the cameras. There are tons of reports of bear destroying trail cameras, regardless of where it was hung in the tree. Somehow the bears find the cameras and destroy them.

There is also the theory that Bigfoot can see in the infrared spectrum, allowing them to easily detect cameras. Heightened smell, superior hearing, combined with incredible vision that can possibly see in the infrared spectrum, are the main reasons most researchers believe there are few trail cam pics. Notice I said few. There are a few that have been made public, but the reason I believe there are not many is because Bigfoot knows they're there. Bigfoot does not live in every forest, therefore the likelihood of crossing paths with one is unlikely. I can promise you though, when you enter the woods where they do live, they know you are there before you get out of your vehicle. Even though they are nocturnal, they live in family groups, and they are always watching. I have 2 separate trail camera stories that happened to my teammate Joe and my teammate Billy.

One night Billy received a notification to his phone that the battery in one of his trail cameras died. He loaded up his four-wheeler and drove to his hunting land. It is 500 acres here in Georgia, surrounded by forest, farms, and a large, beautiful creek. He rides his four-wheeler from the road to the back side of the property. He gets off his four-wheeler and walks down what he described as a "pig trail" to the tree, only to find the camera gone. He was very confused and walked around for about 45 minutes trying to find the camera. He noticed his dog seemed anxious and kept raising its hackles towards something Billy could not see. He gave up and started the walk back to the four-wheeler and guess what was now laying in the "pig trail"? The trail camera. Laid out as if someone wanted to make sure he saw it.

Joe went to his hunting land in east Georgia one day to check on his deer feeders and he noticed one of his trail cameras was not on the tree. He used an app to ping the GPS location of the unit and the camera was no longer on the property. The camera was pinging from deep in a swamp in an area that was not accessible. Joe reached out to the manufacturers of the unit for help. He had them track the location just to make sure something wasn't malfunctioning on his app, and sure enough they determined the camera was definitely deep in the swamp, just as Joe did. Joe was never able to retrieve that camera and said it pinged until the batteries died. I asked him about pictures, and he said he saw some brush and then just blackness, as if the camera was left facing down. I will note Joe had placed the camera about 6ft up the tree, and soon after he found one of his deer feeders in that same area destroyed. The barrel of the feeder had been separated from the legs, and each metal leg was twisted and bent and scattered about.

additional
eyewitness reports

Case File #2

Interview completed 8/4/2020
Eyewitness testimony of a 61-year-old, Army Veteran, served
in the Army from 1979-1987 as a wheeled vehicle mechanic,
resident of Gouverneur, New York. Eyewitness requested to
remain anonymous due to the possibility of public
harassment.

Report 1 (sighting)

Incident Information and Eyewitness Testimony
Year: Estimated year as 1981 or 1982
Location: Army Base, Fort Leonard Wood, Missouri.
Heavily wooded area off a seldom used cut through road.
Area included a ridge and a large cave system.

Time of Year: Late summer or early fall
Time of Day: Approximately 4 p.m.

Questions and Witness' Responses

Were you alone? *"No, there was another G.I. with me. In fact, he got a better look at it than I did."*

When you pulled over did you notice any strange smells or strong odors? *"Didn't smell anything strange, but could hear it going down the embankment breaking branches."*

Did you notice any type of features to tell if it was male or female? *" No, I was more drawn to the face of it, and it didn't really look ape-ish."*

Did you notice if it had a human shaped nose? *"No, because it was kind of turning like it had been looking our way and was turning back to watch where it was going to get out of there". "What color was it? "It was dark brown almost black color. It was a very dark color. On the head you could see there was hair on the side of the head that was very thin looking. You could see the skin underneath it."*

Did it look more like hair or like fur? *"It was long hair It definitely wasn't fur, and it definitely wasn't a bear. There aren't many bears in Missouri at all." Did it maintain a walk or was it kind of running? "It stayed on its back legs. It was definitely bipedal when it went down the hill until it went out of sight."*

Did you notice long arms or cone-shaped head? *"The head was a little bit cone shaped. The arms I didn't pay much attention to, but it kind of had its arms up. They weren't hanging down to the side as we would, kind of 45-degree angle at the elbow."*

Summary of Incident

The witness was a soldier on base and traveling back to his "motor pool" at approximately 4 p.m. one afternoon. He noticed a gate on a cut-through road had been left often due to marching drills that day, so he decided to take the cut-through road to shorten his drive by about three miles. The trip was usually about a seven-mile trip down a road that formed "somewhat of a horseshoe shape" but also contained curves. As the soldier was rounding a curve, he had his head turned talking to a passenger, which was another G.I., when suddenly he saw a creature cross the road in front of him that "looked like an ape". The dark brown creature crossed the road at a walk, with its arms "kinda bent up", within 20 yards of the vehicle, and went down a very steep embankment and into the woods. The creature remained bi-pedal the entire time. The soldier turned to the other G.I. and asked, "did you see that?" The other G.I. acknowledged seeing the creature. They pulled over to the edge of the road where the creature had crossed in an effort to see it more clearly. They could not see the creature because of the thick forest, but the witness reports they could hear it going through the brush, and breaking branches. Witness reports "if it was a bigfoot, I don't think it was an adult one because it wasn't that tall. It was probably about six feet tall. It wasn't overly huge."

Report 2 (Possible Audio Encounter)

Year: Estimated year as 1990
Location: Edwards, New York on Crystal Lake. Heavily wooded area approximately 2 miles off the main road.
Time of Year: Early fall
Time of Day: Approximately 6:30 p.m. "just before dusk, it had started getting dark."

Eyewitness reports he took his father-in-law (who suffered from emphysema), and several of his father-in-law's friends fishing on Crystal Lake in Edwards, New York. He describes the area as a wooded area with parking for the lake approximately two miles off the main road. The trail to the lake is approximately three-fourths of a mile from the parking area. They finished fishing for the day, and the witness was carrying two five-gallon buckets of "Bullheads" back to the truck. Because his father-in-law suffered from emphysema, the witness continued towards the truck while allowing his father-in-law time to stop and rest about every 100 yards or so. His friends would stay behind with the older gentleman, and the eyewitness continued "Because the buckets were getting heavy." Witness reports that when he arrived at the truck the truck was locked, and in front of the truck was a "stunted cedar tree." The tree is described stunted because it had the appearance of growing outwards more so than up.

The witness reports "there was something on the other side of that and it was growling, badly. It was making a heck of a racket, and I had never heard a sound like that before. He reports he was unable to get in the truck because it was locked so he placed the truck between him and whatever was growling. He states, " all of a sudden it started raising heck and all of a sudden all the branches started going crazy" and he thought it was coming through the tree but instead it "let out a roar made the whole stunted cedar shake". When the other men arrived at the vehicle all activity had stopped so there is no other witness to this possible encounter.

Note: The witness states he is not certain if this was a Bigfoot encounter or not, but now he is fascinated with the subject. He states he has learned that apes will hit brush in an effort to scare invaders when they are guarding their territory, and he has often wondered if that was what happened in this case. He reports he does not believe this was an encounter with a bear because usually bears will growl and have an odor. He reports no odors with this encounter.

How have this affected you? Witness reports he was once "on the fence", but now is a believer because He watched the unknown creature cross the road in front of his vehicle in 1981. He reports he is leerier when he goes into the woods but is always armed due to the high bear population in upstate New York.

What do you think Bigfoot is? *"I think it is a descendant of Gigantopithecus that came across on the land bridge.*

There are just too many sightings and some good videos out there. Of course some are bogus, but some you just can't explain."

"All of a Sudden, I Did Not Want to Be There Anymore"

"There is a place on Flint River that my dad always took me to as a kid. We camped and fished there, and it was a comforting place to me. One morning I decided to drive out to this place to sit and meditate and think about my future. I was feeling down that day for whatever reason, and I needed to think about my future as a young man. It was in 1988, and I was 19 years old at the time. It was a grey, cloudy, wet, and cold February day. I drove my truck near the mouth of Pigeon Creek. I had been sitting there for maybe 40-45 minutes pitching pebbles into the river and thinking about my life when I looked down the river.

For whatever reason something made me look across the river. I saw something coming up through the woods. I could see the movement but didn't think much of it. I figured it was a deer or something, but as it got closer it appeared to be a person except it was all very dark. I could tell it did not have any clothes on. It was like a deep charcoal brown color, and I could tell it was walking on two legs, so I assumed it was a person. My first thoughts were that it was a very tall, slim, naked, very dark-skinned man. I thought to myself, "why would a person be way down in the woods like this on a cold dreary day without any clothes on and on the Flint River"?

At that time, Bigfoot was not on my mind. My mind was having a hard time processing what I was seeing. I had watched a few TV shows that talked about a large hairy creature that lived out in the western Rockies or southern Canada. My mind could not put it together because I did not know I was supposed to see "that" here.

Once it was directly across the river from me, I noticed its gait, and it had its head slightly down. It was just swinging its arms and it looked like the back went up to massive shoulders, no neck, and what looked like a conical shaped head. It was then I could see hair swaying off the back of the forearms and off the back of the legs. This thing was walking like it was on its way somewhere, and I was able to watch it walk just as far up the river as I had watched it come from down the river. There were no leaves on the trees that time of year, and I could see a long way through the woods.

After it walked past me and out of sight is when I started to get scared and shook up. I started thinking, "are there more or are there some on this side of the river." All of a sudden, I did not want to be there anymore, and I left. I just dismissed it from my mind because I could not really determine what I had seen.

Some years later I learned about the Elkins Creek cast and boom, it all started to make sense to me. That's the only time I have ever seen it. I still fish and hunt and I still go to that spot to hunt. I am not afraid to be there, but I am very aware there's a lot more going on in the woods than the average person thinks.

"My name is Curt Ousley and I know what I saw that day."

Report taken 11/28/2023
Location of sighting-Manchester, Georgia

"I Could Feel the Breath of That Thing on My Neck"

As a child, I overheard "the grown folks" talking, and my uncle was sharing a story from his childhood that has stuck with me for the past 45 years. I was about ten when I first heard this story. This incident has crossed my mind many times, and I finally decided to give him a call to learn more about what happened that night. In 45 years, the story hasn't changed, and it's stories like this that make me believe there's a lot of weird stuff that happens in Heard County, Georgia. As a matter of fact, I've learned first-hand that strange things do happen there.

Due to the usual harassment people often endure when they share stories or experiences other people don't want to believe, he has taken my advice and will remain anonymous at this time. The following story is something that he remembers from his childhood, and it was discussed amongst his family members for many years. The witness is a 72-year-old man, retired, and a native of Heard County. He currently resides in Heard County, along with many extended family members. Here is the incident as he remembers it.

"It was about 1954, and I remember it happening. My daddy's youngest brother was about 20 years old. He hadn't been married for long, and they were living in one of my grandmother's houses. We called it 'The Little House.' We lived on Pea Ridge Road, and we were living in my grandmother's other house. I think she was living in Coweta County at the time. My uncle loved to hunt, and we always had a bunch of coon dogs. One night he came home from work, and it was already dark. We didn't have electricity back then, so his wife had already gone to bed. He ate his dinner, took off his shoes, and was getting ready to go to bed himself when he heard his coon dogs raising cane. He told us later; it had sounded like they had treed something in the woods behind his house. He put his shoes back on, grabbed his gun, and went behind the house. He said he called the dogs, and they just got louder. He walked into the woods towards Hwy 27, and he said every time he'd start getting close to the dogs, they'd start running again until they sounded like they'd treed something again. He said this happened several times, until they were deep into the woods, and he eventually came to an old pulpwood road. He was standing in the middle of the old road when his dogs came running back towards him and ran past him. It was then he heard limbs cracking and popping, and he said he could hear something huge coming through the trees towards him. He took off running as fast as he could. He ran out of the woods not too far from his house, but he was so scared and running so hard, that he didn't even slow down at his own house. He said he could feel the creature on his heels as he was running. He ran past his house and crashed through the front door of our house. Our house didn't have a porch on it, and back then no one locked their doors at night. He crashed through the door, slammed it shut, and squatted up against the wall. He could hear his dogs under the house raising cane, and he finally got up the nerve to crawl over to one of the windows beside the door. We had a long window on each side of the door, and he raised up just enough to look out. He said what he saw that night scared him to death. It was a large hairy black-looking creature that had chased him on two legs. He said it was huge, and he could see it in the moonlight standing on the edge of the woods. I specifically remember him saying, 'I could feel the breath of that thang on my neck.' He stayed there for quite a while, until the dogs settled down, and eventually he ran home.

The Pea Ridge Road Monster

Heard County, Georgia
January 5, 2025

Due to the number of reported sightings and encounters I have been privy to, I have decided to dig a little deeper into what locals call, "The Pea Ridge Road Monster." I assumed this creature would be one of the Bigfoot creatures that I believe live in that area, but after today's interview I am second guessing that. One of the last things he told me in today's interview was, "if you decide to go looking for this creature, you're going to wish you hadn't." Those words are now burned into my brain, and now I really don't know if I want to go looking for this creature. He told me exactly where to go and what time to be there to possibly get a glimpse of this creature. Of course that is assuming the creature is still in the area.

I did a report last year titled, "I Could Feel the Breath of that Thing on my Neck." It described a coon hunter that was chased from the woods, down Pea Ridge Road, and into his brother's house to escape the creature. It followed him so close he could feel it breathing on his neck, and once inside the house he got a glimpse of a tall black creature covered in hair standing in the wood line. This encounter happened in the 50's, and today's witness encountered the creature during the 80's. Could this be the same creature, or are there generations of these creatures living in the woods on Pea Ridge Road?

The witness has asked to remain anonymous. He told me he would like to just leave this whole chapter of his life behind him and has tried to forget about the years he spent on Pea Ridge Road. I won't go into a lot of detail about all the things he shared with me today regarding his home life, so I will just say he did not grow up in a happy healthy home. He spent most of his time outside, away from his stepfather. He would either be in the woods or visiting neighbors up and down the country road. He told me he would sleep in the woods sometimes to avoid going inside his home. He contributes his lack of fear of the dark woods and encounters with the creature to the abusive environment of his childhood.

I plan to complete an investigation of some other things we discussed today, so hopefully I will be able to access some old police reports and meet with some of the same families that still live on Pea Ridge Road. It is my intent to follow up on all these leads and continue this investigation until all my resources have been exhausted.

For the sake of keeping the witness' identity secret, I am going to call him Tom. Tom told me he was about eight years old when he moved to Pea Ridge Road with his mother, brother, and stepfather, and he lived there until he was 14-15 years old. The more time Tom spent in the woods, and walking the dark country roads at night, the more comfortable he became. He reports that he saw the creature on multiple occasions, and the main thing he can remember is its eyes. He says the first time he saw the creature he thought it was just a skinny bear with strange glowing yellow eyes. He didn't really know much about bears, and being a young kid, he just assumed bears were in the area. He saw it a few times, but one night he got a much closer look. He saw it walking on two legs and could clearly see its face. It was then he could see the face of a dog. Apparently, the creature knew that

Tom would often walk at night, and it would follow Tom. Tom said that a few times he tried to get closer to the creature, but the creature would move away, never allowing Tom to get less than 30 yards from it. Tom says the creature never tried to bother him, just followed him and watched him. Just being a kid, and considering Tom's homelife, he says he often wondered if the creature was a demon or a guardian angel. It was just a very confusing time in his life.

Tom recalls one night walking down Thompson Road, which is a narrow dirt road that turns off Pea Ridge Road. Several people lived on Thompson Road, and even though it was a narrow dirt road, it was still a well-traveled road. Tom says the creature followed him for several hours but was much faster than he was because it would cross the road numerous times in front of him and behind him, with just one giant step across the road. Tom says at times he would run as fast as he could, but the creature was able to continue circling him regardless of his speed.

I asked Tom to describe exactly what the creature looked like. He told me all he could ever really do was look into its eyes. He does remember it was a very dark color, maybe dark brown/black. He does not remember ever seeing a tail and cannot remember the legs or the arms in detail. He can remember the face, and that it "stunk like hell". It had the face of a dog with glowing yellowish orange eyes, and it smelled like it had been urinating on itself over and over. He does remember seeing it standing at the corner of a neighbor's house one night and estimates the height to have been 12 feet tall.

He recalls a fatal car accident on the road one night. He was in the woods watching the police work the scene. A vehicle had flipped, and it was assumed the driver had run off the road and overcorrected. Tom says he was watching all the lights, etc., when he saw the creature in the road in the distance. The creature was watching as if the driver had swerved to avoid hitting it, and it had caused the accident. (There is a more to this part that will be covered in Part 2 which gave Tom this impression)

Tom also recalls a neighbor hitting something in the road one night with her car, that was carrying a buck deer in its mouth. Luckily, she was able to keep driving and she didn't stop until she was home. A few days later Tom watched the wrecker load the car which was basically destroyed. Tom remembers her husband finding two different types of hairs in the damage. One type was obviously deer, but no one could determine what the other hairs were from.

Hunters Have Possible Bigfoot Sighting in Heard County, Georgia

If you have been following along with my previous reports about "The Pea Ridge Road Monster", then you need to know that this sighting happened just a few miles away. I have a map of where both incidents occurred, but at this time I cannot reveal the locations due to ongoing research.

You will just have to trust me when I tell you the two locations are quite close to Pea Ridge Road, especially "as the crow flies."

This witness requested to be anonymous, like most do. The good thing about this witness is that I have personally known him for a long time, and I know he would not come to me with this information if it wasn't true. He has carried this memory with him for over 20 years, and he has never been able to share it with anyone out of fear of ridicule. I will be so glad when the day comes and so many people can say, "I told you so." It's sad when honorable trustworthy people are called liars or crazy.

For this report, I will call this witness Mark. Mark is in his 50's, married with children, an experienced hunter and outdoorsman, and has an honorable reputation. I can find no reason not to believe every detail of his experiences. One of his experiences only involved some guttural growling he couldn't recognize, and intense shaking of whole trees by a creature he could not see while he was in his deer stand early one morning. This event happened at a different location than the actual sighting, but also not more than a few miles from Pea Ridge Road.

Mark explained to me that it was March 2005, and he and his stepfather had leased some private property to hunt for several years and hunted often. It was turkey season, so they went into a field and set up their blind and began the wait. Mark describes sitting there for a short period of time, when they both saw movement to their right. His first thought was another hunter was trespassing and wearing a ghillie suit, but after a few seconds of disbelief he realized that was not what he was looking at.

He states he and his stepfather both watched a brownish, hairy, and quite lanky creature walk from the tree line on two legs, cross the field, walk within six feet of a grazing deer that paid it no attention, and faded away into the woods again. He says the creature was walking like it had somewhere to go and obviously never knew the men were there.

He sat there in disbelief and just looked at this stepfather. He says the only comment his stepfather made about the whole ordeal was, "I don't think we need to tell anybody about this", and they never spoke of it again. This reaction is commonly reported. We all react differently to different situations, and I personally think it is harder for men sometimes to come forward when they see things that they cannot explain. People will often question themselves about what they saw because their brain just cannot process it, so they just tuck the memory away as a coping mechanism.

Unfortunately, Mark's stepfather has passed away, but Mark says the details of that event are still vivid in his mind. He reports no smell, and he specifically remembers it was a windy day. He believes that is why the creature never smelled them. The creature appeared to be about seven feet tall, walked with a slight forward bend, and its arms appeared longer than a human. He says the creature just looked forward and walked with a purpose.

"It's Been 38 Years, and the Pea Ridge Road Monster Still Exists"

Heard County, Georgia

I have lived on Pea Ridge Road all my life, and my family has been on this road for several generations. My grandfather used to make moonshine and would talk about a creature that lived down in the swamp. When we told our Pawpaw what we saw that day, he said "I told y'all he was down there." A lot of people think it's a panther, but what we saw that day was no panther. This was many years ago, when I was only 10-12 years old, but there is no mistaking what my cousin and I both saw that day.

Even though that was about 38 years ago, a creature still lives here. I know for sure it comes back every spring at least. It may not be the same creature. It may be its offspring or something, but there is no mistaking it's scream. The best way I can describe it is that it sounds like a large animal and an old woman at the same time, and no it's not a large cat. This thing responds back to the coyotes. You will hear the coyotes, and then way off in the distance you will hear this thing scream.

My cousin and I had dirt bikes, and we were out riding that day. There is an old cut-through road from Pearidge to Thompson Road, kind of like an old pulpwood road. We were just riding down that road and a creature crossed the road just eight-to-ten feet in front of us. We both saw it. It was about five-to-six feet tall, walking on two legs, with greyish black hair. We did not see its face, just its body. We freaked out and didn't stop. We finally got up the nerve to go back the next day to look for tracks, but we didn't find anything. Anybody that went to school with us back then should remember this story because we told everyone at school. As a matter of fact, we are the ones that originally started calling it the "Pea Ridge Road Monster."

I will tell you something else. My uncle lived on Thompson Road, and back then there were just a handful of houses on that road. His pasture was down from his house near the swamp and an old beaver pond. One night something got into his pasture and killed two goats and a calf by biting or cutting their throats. It didn't eat the animals; it just tore open their throats and left them.

My name is Andy Elkins, and I do not mind using my name for this report. I know what I saw that day, and I have talked about it since. Anybody that went to school with me and my cousin should remember because we told the whole school. If anyone wants to talk with me about it, I will tell them just like I am telling you. If there were any families around here at the time that didn't know about the creature, it's because they stayed to themselves and never spent anytime outside at night.

Interviewed on 1/10/2025

Note: The Elkins family was one of the families that "Tom" from a previous report recommended I find to interview. I was lucky enough to make that happen and will continue the search for more information.

"It Had the Face of an Old Woman"

Heard County, Georgia

The following is a short report, and just a creepy story a friend of mine shared with a group of us cowgirls one night. At the time, there was a group of five-to-six of us women that rode horses together a lot. When I say a lot, I mean we ate, slept, and breathed horses. It was a wonderful time in my life, and we have all remained friends. It is our dream to ride together again someday. Those were some fantastic years that I still cherish, and we all loved to hang out at my little barn.

One night we were sitting around talking, and my friend I will call "Lisa" for the sake of this story, shared something with us that still creeps us out. Now, no one is saying this was or was not anything, but since it did happen in Heard County, I feel compelled to include this story in my reports.

Lisa worked at the Ryans Steakhouse in LaGrange, Ga. She worked the night shift as a waitress and had agreed to drive the night manager home due to his car being in the shop. The restaurant stayed open late, and the night-crew always had a lot of cleaning and stocking to do before they could leave. It was after midnight before they were able to lock up and leave for the night. They took Hwy 219 (Mooty Bridge Road) towards the manager's home in Heard County.

They had just crossed over into Heard County when suddenly there was something or someone lying in the road. Lisa said she did not see it until she was right on it, and she had no time to brake. It took up her entire lane and looked like it was belly-crawling very slowly. According to Lisa, it had dark coarse hair in patches, and she could also see it had dark colored skin. Just before impact it turned its head, and then she felt like it looked into her eyes. Lisa said it had the face of an old woman with "long straggly hair on its head and wrinkles on its face."

Lisa drove a small sedan, and she said the impact was hard, and she could feel the creature under her car as she drove over it. Of course, they both freaked out, and she turned around to see what she had hit, and nothing was there. Once they arrived at her manager's house, he was able to look under her car and remove a large chuck of flesh with long black hairs attached. The manager told Lisa he had seen a lot of animals, but he had no idea what they had just ran over. She said it tore her car up underneath, but didn't do any visible damage to the outside or cause any driving issues.

"It Sounded Like Chanting or Someone Mumbling Very Low in an Unknown Language"

I just got off the phone with two of the four men that experienced something very strange about ten years ago in Heard County. This is probably one of the creepiest stories I have personally been told. I like to investigate Bigfoot, period. I don't want to know about ghosts, Dogman, portals, UFOs, orbs, etc., yet sometimes these stories are unavoidable. You can ask any researcher, and they will tell you that you cannot research Bigfoot and ignore all the paranormal reports. There are too many reports of paranormal activities surrounding Bigfoot sightings or known hotspots of Bigfoot activity.

Due to the risk of public harassment and ridicule, I am going to keep the identity of both witnesses confidential at this time. One of the men, a 60 yr. old college-educated professional, has asked to remain anonymous due to his career, but the other witness did give me permission to use his name. I know how cruel some people can be when witnesses come forward, so I am going to keep both names confidential at this time. I am also going to keep the exact location of this incident confidential for now. My team and I are researching what is known as the "Troup-Heard Corridor", and we still have a lot of investigating to do in some of these areas. I will say this incident happened south of Franklin, Ga. and east of the Chattahoochee River. This story is written as the combined perspectives of both men that were interviewed separately:

"It was about 2015, and we had some hunting property that was adjacent to the Chattahoochee River. We had been hunting that property two-three years prior to this incident, and we decided to go coyote hunting one night. This was private land with only one way in and out. The property had a locked gate where we would enter from the road, and on this particular night there were four of us in two separate trucks. Once we got through the gate, we locked it behind us and drove a couple of miles and parked. We got out of the truck, made some calls like the 'dying rabbit' and some others, but we did not hear anything.

After a little while, we got back in the trucks and went about three more miles into the woods. We parked again, got out and made some more calls. We were sitting on a hillside where we could see down the road, but we never heard anything. We were not getting any responses from the coyotes that night. We were there a couple of hours I guess when we saw what looked like a flashlight, but then it looked like headlights coming down the road. We just assumed it was the game warden. We were the only ones back there, so it had to be the 'the man' coming to check us out. The lights stayed about waist high and three-to-four feet apart, and when they got a lot closer to us, they went out. It looked like the game warden had turned his headlights off, so we decided to just walk to where he was. We thought it was kind of weird he didn't pull up to where we were because it was obvious we were there. We had spotlights going and were armed to the max.

We walked to where we thought the game warden was parked, ready to show him our license and information but there was no one there. We were quite confused and decided he must have parked further away than we realized. We walked back to the trucks and then drove about three miles back. As we were driving, we thought we would see the game warden, but that never happened. The game warden was nowhere to be found.

We parked the trucks again and got out. We were baffled and very confused as to why we saw those headlights, yet there was no vehicle to be found. That was the only road going in and out of the property, not to mention a locked gate at the road. Where we were parked, it was kind of like a ridge. It went uphill on the left side of the road, and it went downhill on the right side, and both were kind of steep. The whole area was thickly covered in young pines that were about eight-to-ten feet tall.

We were just standing there talking when suddenly there was a flash of blue light. I cannot explain to you how bright and huge this blue flash was. It was as if it came up from the hillside we had originally been sitting on, and as it went up it got wider. The whole area was lit up in a bright neon blue. It was an absolute explosion of blue light like a bomb, but there was no sound. Out of instinct we ducked as if two planes had collided overhead or something, but there was silence all around. We closed the tailgates and got our guns.

We were in awe just looking around trying to figure out what had just happened, when to our left we heard something that sounded like low mumbling. We couldn't make out what they were saying, and it almost sounded like chanting. Then it looked like someone ignited a small fire. It was literally only about ten yards away from us, and we could see the silhouette of what looked like people circling the fire. It sounded like chanting or someone mumbling very low in an unknown language. We couldn't make out any features, only that it was a small flame about 1 foot tall, and what looked like three-to-four people circling the flame mumbling something that sounded almost ritualistic.

Then suddenly the flame disappeared and immediately appeared on the opposite side of the road, but this time it was about ten yards away and downhill from us. It was the exact same mumbling/chanting, and the exact same type of circling a flame. Man, we freaked out and got the hell out of there."

I asked the gentlemen if they continued to hunt there. One said he never went back again despite having hunted that land two-to-three years prior, but the other said he did go back about two weeks later to deer hunt in the daytime. He said it was the very end of the day, and he only had about 30 minutes of legal daylight left, so he climbed a tree stand just to use up the last few minutes. He said he was up in that tree stand for about 20 minutes when he heard it. He heard that same low ritualistic chatter they had all heard a few weeks prior, so he hurried down and left.

Report taken on 4/23/2025

If you're familiar with my search for eyewitness testimonies and stories about the Pea Ridge Road Monster in Heard Co, Georgia, then you're going to enjoy this woman's own story she has been kind enough to send to me. I now have all three of her encounter stories, two are passed down through the generations and one she experienced herself. She is a gifted writer, and the only changes I make will be to a few names and a few locations that need to remain confidential at this time for research purposes. Thank you, Mary Thompson, for these incredible encounter stories. This one actually reminds me of the little boy in North Carolina that disappeared for a few days from his backyard and was returned. He told his family a bear took care of him in the below freezing temps. Look it up if you don't remember. It was Jan 2019 I believe. Easy google search.

"Hi! Here is My First Story"

Spring 1932

My grandparents, Sally and Ripley Breed, were married in Alabama in 1925, and their oldest son, Melvin, was born in 1927. By 1932, they lived on ******* Road, near Franklin.

One day, my granny, who had two more small boys and was pregnant with her oldest daughter, took all of them to a neighbor's house to wash some sheets. The women got busy and lost track of the kids, but at some point Melvin wandered off. They looked for him, couldn't find him, and sent one of the older children to another neighbor to get more help. People began to gather, a search party was organized, and everyone looked until dark. The search began again as soon as it was daylight. During the afternoon, a man drove up with Melvin in his car. He had found him next to the highway a little north of Five Points. Melvin said a hairy man had taken him from the back yard. Since he was only 5, everyone thought either he was making it up, or that he had possibly been snatched by a bear. After he was grown, however, he had a few more details. He had gone a little way into the woods when a large man covered in brown hair had suddenly picked him up by the back of his shirt. He insisted it was a man, not a bear. It smelled like pee and had light yellow eyes. Melvin was too scared to scream or fight. The man carried him a long way, until they came to a small stream. Hiding in the bushes were 3 more of these things. One was an adult female, holding a baby as big as Melvin, and a smaller one he thought was a boy. Mama Thing immediately began arguing with Daddy Thing by growling, snorting, and huffing. Daddy Thing argued back a while before tossing Melvin on the ground and heading off into the woods again. Mama Thing ignored him, but Boy Thing came over and began poking at him. Melvin just sat and cried, wanting to go home. After a while Daddy Thing came back with what might have been part of a deer and tried to get him to eat it, but he couldn't. The rest of the family ate it, and when it got dark, Mama and Daddy Thing put him and the other children between them and went to sleep. Melvin was too scared to try to run away. The next morning, Daddy Thing tried to feed him more raw meat, and Mama and Daddy Thing had another fight, this one involving some screeching and shoving. Finally, Daddy Thing grabbed Melvin by the back of his shirt again and began walking through the woods. They walked a very long time until they came to the highway. Daddy Thing shoved Melvin toward the road and disappeared. To the end of his days, Uncle Melvin insisted he had been kidnapped by a hairy man, refusing to even say the word 'Bigfoot'."

Mary's 2nd Encounter Story

Here is the 2nd Encounter story of the possible Pea Ridge Road Monster that was sent to me by Mary Thompson, a lifelong resident of Heard County, Ga. I have left the story just as Mary sent to me, but I did change some of the names as requested. These encounters occurred in what is now known as the "Troup Heard Corridor", where a lot of strangeness is reported, including Bigfoot, UFOs, and Orbs. The THC actually reaches further than Troup and Heard County. It extends into parts of Alabama and several other Georgia counties.

"Summer 1953"

This took place shortly after my mom's 8th birthday, so the end of July/beginning of August, 1953. At that time, the Breed family was living on Boise Road off Hwy 27. In addition to my grandparents, the children remaining at home were Julian, 12, Fannie, 10, my mother, Maggie, 8, John, 6, and Ethan, 4. My grandfather was not a very nice man. He often got drunk and abused my grandmother, so she and the children had worked out a system. When my grandfather started to act ugly, the older children were to quietly grab a quilt and a younger child, and head for the woods. My granny would join them as soon as she could, and they would spend the night hiding from Grandpa. This particular night, he got between them and the woods, so they circled around to the big pasture next to Hwy 27. Just down the hill from where the big Blossman gas tank later sat was a cattle feed box. Basically, it was a rectangular wooden box on legs with a tin roof. There was some hay in it at the time, so they put one quilt down to sleep on and had one more to put over them. My mother, grandmother, and aunt were sleeping at one end, and my three uncles at the other. It was a tight fit, but other than that it was comfortable, so after a while they all fell asleep. Sometime in the night, my mother woke up to hear Uncle Julian say, "Just be still, and it won't hurt us." She started to sit up, but my granny pulled her back down and told her to be quiet. Mom immediately thought Grandpa had found them. Her head was on Granny's chest, and she could hear her heart beating really fast. She turned her head a little and saw someone walking around the feed box. It was not Grandpa. It was way too tall, for one thing, and it stunk like a soured pig pen. Also, it was making grunting and sniffing sounds, whereas Grandpa tended to yell and scream. It didn't reach inside or bend down for a closer look. After circling them a few times, it headed for the top of the hill. Mom then sat up and watched it until it went into the woods. It had the shape of a man. but she couldn't see any clothes. She remembered her brother and mother discussing whether they should leave where they were, but Uncle Julian pointed out that whatever the thing was, it could have hurt them already if it wanted to. They sat there and whispered about it for a while, sort of comparing notes. The only one who slept through it all was four-year-old Ethan. Everyone else got at least a quick look at whatever it was, and all agreed it wasn't a man. All of them smelled something nasty, but everyone seemed to smell something different. Uncle Julian said he just 'knew' they weren't in any real danger. It was surprised and puzzled to find a bunch of people in the feed box, but it had no intent to harm them, and after deciding they weren't going to harm it, he went on his way. They spent the rest of the night there, and the thing didn't come back. As far as I know, none of them ever had such an encounter again. I once asked Uncle Julian how he knew they weren't in danger, but all he said was that he didn't want to talk about it."

Mary's 3rd Encounter Story

The 3rd and final encounter story sent to me by Mary Thompson. The 1st two were encounters that her mother, uncles, and great uncles discussed through the generations, but this last story is Mary's. Again, I had to remove some information to avoid giving out too much information for now, so I apologize for that. I have really enjoyed reading her stories, and I hope you have as well. I hope these eyewitness reports and stories I have been sharing will continue to encourage more witnesses to come forward.

"June 1982"

So, this takes place on Thompson Road close to Five Points. At that time, it was still called Pea Ridge Road. For reasons I'd rather not go into, I pretty much found myself living alone in the woods at age 15. I had built a hut/treehouse about a quarter mile from my family's home, and if my mom wasn't around, that's where I was, with my dog and a .22 rifle. My dog was a collie/shepherd/mutt mix named Mike, who weighed about 50 pounds, and was fiercely protective of me. He was my best buddy, and I built him a sort of elevator to get him up into the treehouse, which was on top of a pretty large hill. (Someone has since built a real house in almost the same spot.) Down below on the west side was an empty pasture with Fromby Creek running across one corner; the other 3 sides were woods. I have never been afraid of being in the woods after dark. Hell, I used to carry a 10-

pound portable TV and a 20-pound car battery over a mile away to watch 'Starsky and Hutch' reruns. Most critters truly are more afraid of you than you need to be of them. This particular night was hot, so I folded back the big piece of canvas I used as a roof, hoping for a stray breeze. I had an old army cot to sleep on in one corner, and Mike slept on a piece of carpet beside my bed. I kept my rifle, unloaded, under my bed, but within reach. The treehouse was basically a big rectangle with a hip-high railing made of branches and chicken wire. We were only about 12 feet off the ground, but the hill sloped away on 2 sides, meaning an actual drop of about 30 or more feet straight down. (I hope this makes sense.) I woke up during the night when Mike started growling. At first, I told him to hush, but he didn't, and soon he got up to pace back and forth. I sat up in bed, groggy, and listened. Down at the bottom of the hill on the pasture side, something was moving in the undergrowth. My first thought was deer, but Mike never growled at deer. I had candles, lanterns, and flashlights, but didn't want a light to give away my position, so for a few minutes I just sat and listened, trying to wake myself up. Whatever it was came closer, and sounded pretty big. Mike was getting more agitated, and when I reached out to touch him, he jerked away to keep pacing. I had raised him from a puppy, and realized he was going into 'I'll rip your throat out if you get too close to my mama!' mode and wondered if I should load my rifle. One of those reasons I didn't sleep at home anymore might be headed my way. I leaned over the side of the bed to get the gun, and Mike put his front paws on the edge of the bed. I thought, "Shit, this might be a bear!" There were some around, though I had not laid eyes on one in years. 2 things suddenly happened at once. First, a breeze came from the pasture, and I smelled something so rank I almost puked. It was like hot garbage somebody had been pooping and peeing in for days. Second, Mike launched himself over me and was going across the railing. I instantly grabbed him around the middle as he went into a barking frenzy. Several thoughts went through my head at once, and they weren't mine. As best I can remember: 'Dog, big dog, here? supposed to be at them's, no dog here before, dog hurt, hurt dog, go back, water, go down.'

I was nauseous and dizzy, and Mike and I both almost went over the railing, but my shoulder hit and stopped us. Let me tell you, your headspace being invaded, especially unexpectedly, will put you through some changes. I dimly remember getting one arm between Mike's front legs and around his neck before throwing us both to the floor and lying on him. I've always been a big gal, but it was still a struggle. He was absolutely beyond pissed, I thought I had finally lost what mind I did have, and for a while all I could do was lay on top of my dog and pant for breath. When Mike stopped busting my eardrums barking, I sat up but kept both arms wrapped around him. I didn't let go until he settled down to growling again. He went to the far end of the treehouse and stood there with his hair raised. I realized I couldn't hear movement down the hill anymore and groped around until I found a flashlight. My mental state could be described as

'HOLY SH*T, WHAT THE **** JUST HAPPENED?' I wasn't scared. That was weird, but truly the only time I felt fear was when I thought Mike was going to jump down and hurt himself. Now that he had calmed, my biggest worry was whether I had had a stroke or aneurysm or something. I thought about what Uncle Julian had said, knowing that the hairy man thing wasn't going to hurt anybody, and understood why he didn't want to talk about it. I certainly didn't want to at that moment, and who was going to believe me anyway? I spent the rest of the night sitting on the floor with my loaded rifle in my lap, trying to make sense of things. The next day, I went to the other 2 uncles that had the 1953 encounter, but they weren't much help. There is this thing among some Native American tribes, including the Blackfeet I'm descended from, that to speak of something is to draw it to you. Their advice was don't think about it, da*n sure don't talk about it, and try to forget it even happened. I haven't been able to do that, more than 40 years later. I didn't want to go looking for whatever it was I heard and smelled, but I don't think I'd be frightened to come across it accidentally again. I have worked out a few theories of sorts over the years. These things, whatever people decide to call them, definitely exist. A cluster of them lived (REDACTED), their home territory was (REDACTED). They roam around mostly in spring and summer, when (REDACTED). If you look at a map, these things could be the Pea Ridge Road Monster, and I'm willing to bet there are far more encounters than people admit. They don't like getting wet, but use waterways to navigate. They do not like dogs, and dogs don't like them. They don't want to interact with humans, but don't want to hurt or scare us if it can be avoided. I still can't get my brain around why I heard something else's thoughts in my head, but it might go back to being part Blackfoot. My tribe paid a lot of attention to dreams and visions in the past, and it could be related. Growing up in the THC, there is no end to the 'high strangeness'; at 58 years old, I'm over it :). I hope this helps, and you can use my name. Most people who know me think I'm nuts already. Like Dr. Seuss said, "Those who mind don't matter, and those who matter don't mind."

Two Different Witnesses, Two Different Events, Too Coincidental

LaGrange, Ga. Troup County

In August 2024, I was chatting with a gentleman that lives in North Georgia. We were of course discussing Bigfoot, and he told me he saw one in 2020 in LaGrange. When he told me where, I honestly wasn't all that surprised because several of the reports I have taken are in that same general area.

Being from North Georgia, he wasn't familiar with the area and his family rented a lodge for a weekend from VRBO. The lodge was rented for the purpose of a weekend family reunion, and they were trying to rent something close to West Point Lake. The lodge has a pond on the property and is somewhat secluded and surrounded by 18 wooded acres.

He told me he was sitting on the lower deck in the back of the house smoking two Boston butts when he saw something move about seventy yards away. Due to the angle of the sun, he was able to see through the trees close to the pond. That is where he saw it standing. He told me he was able to see a face, shoulder, and arm hanging down. The creature was covered in chestnut colored hair, and he could also see one leg. He stared at the creature in the wood line for about two minutes and it never moved. Then his phone dinged, and he looked down at his phone, and when he looked back up the creature was gone.

He was able to give me the information about this location, and I was not aware LaGrange had this beautiful lodge before this interview. The location of the sighting is a place called "Creek Lodge." You can find it online, and the address is 1351 New Franklin Road, LaGrange, Ga. It's a beautiful place and now I really want to rent it haha. Well, I stored this report in my memory bank and after speaking with another witness a few days ago, I was able to make the connection.

I had posted a report about the "Pea Ridge Road Monster" and it seemed to get a lot of attention. It was shared multiple times, and I received a few messages from some of its readers. This is often the case and one of the main reasons I share my reports. One gentleman sent me a message and asked if I would call him. He stated he had a really short story, but it was something that would impact him forever. We scheduled a time to talk, and he not only told me what happened that night, but he has given me permission to use his name. Thank you, Jonathan H., for reaching out to me.

Jonathan did not have a sighting, but he did experience something very strange one night. He told me what happened, and when he told me the location, I remembered the sighting at the lodge. As the crow flies, Jonathan was approximately 1000 yards from the lodge when he had his possible encounter.

Jonathan explained that he and a buddy had been out crappie fishing all day and were just standing at the edge of his backyard talking when they heard it. It was a growl so low and guttural that it reverberated through their bodies. The growl, that he can only describe as what a T-Rex would sound like, came from the creek that was about 100 yards away. He described it as a subtle but intense growl that he knew came from the creek, but at the same time it felt like it was right in front of them because they could feel it. It only growled once, but he said they both knew it was a warning, as if a creature was telling them "Do not get any closer." He said they both looked at each other in shock and ran into the house. They got flashlights and went back to look around but did not see anything.

Even though the men did not see anything, he says it was just a sound and a feeling that he cannot explain, and it will impact him for the rest of his life. He still goes into the woods there to hunt, but the whole time he is there he thinks about just how large a creature that had to be in the woods that night, and he worries that it may still be around.

Date of report 1/17/2025

"It Felt Like My Bones Were Rattling."

Troup County, Georgia

"It was an extremely cold winter day in 1975 when I had my experience. I remember the year because I was 12 years old, and my dad gave me a youth 20-gauge single-shot shotgun. I wanted to go hunting really bad, but my dad wasn't a hunter. He was the pastor of Mountville Baptist Church at the time. He liked to fish, but he never did hunt. There were two men in the church named Ronnie and James, and they agreed to take me squirrel hunting one morning. James was an Apache Indian, and he always wore a big Bowie Knife on his side. I remember how cold it was that morning because I was so new to hunting that I had to wear my tennis shoes and two pairs of socks. I remember freezing, but I was so pumped to finally get to go hunting that I didn't care. I remember we went out Mountville-Hogansville Road until we got to a wooden bridge. (Determined during the interview he is referring to Beech Creek) We crossed the bridge, parked on the right side of the road, walked across the road, and crossed the bridge to enter the woods on the left side of the creek. The creek back then was about eight feet wide and deep. The plan was to walk down the creek for a while and then turn around and walk back out. We had been walking for a while, and I had about 10-12 squirrels in my backpack. The guys would walk ahead of me and shake vines or whatever, and I would shoot the squirrels. We were walking along when James suddenly stopped and said, 'y'all stop. I will be right back.' James walked up to a pine thicket, and I asked Ronnie what was going on and he said, 'we are being stalked.' I figured it was some kind of a set up to try to scare me since it was my first time hunting, but then a limb came through the trees and landed behind us. First, I thought maybe it had fallen, but then I realized it had actually slid when it hit the ground and pushed up leaves. A falling limb is not going to slide across the ground. James was still up there, and he kept stopping and looking as he walked back to where we were. James led us to a tree that had fallen across the creek, and I remember him saying he could hear a low chatter and breathing so we needed to cross over to put the creek between it and us. I remember him saying that specifically because I wanted to know what 'it' was. We started walking back to the truck when we heard something coming down through those woods that sounded like a tank, and it jumped into that creek. The splash was so loud it sounded like a car had fallen in the creek. It was as if he was intentionally smashing stuff just so we would hear him. I could hear it wading around in the water, and I could tell it was on two feet walking around. Then I heard it jump from the water to the top of a five-six-foot embankment and it grunted when it jumped. Ronnie was just standing there speechless, and James pulled out his knife. All of a sudden, a 30-foot-tall cedar tree just started shaking back and forth, and that thing let out a howl that I cannot explain. It felt like my soul left my body. It felt like my bones were rattling. James grabbed the squirrels I had shot and tossed them on the ground and told me to head straight for the truck and he would keep up the rear. He told me to throw my gun in the back and get inside the cab quickly. As soon as I hit the road that thing screamed again, and Ronnie and James came running out of the woods. Then a large rock landed in front of the truck. Ronnie jumped in the driver's side and said, 'what was that?' I believe James said it was a Nik'inla'eena', but I can't be certain. I was just so scared I barely heard what he said. When we drove off, we were so upset that Ronnie drove all the way to Bass Crossroads, and we took Hwy 29 back to LaGrange. They would not even turn around and drive back over the bridge to go home. Whatever it was that morning, it stayed on the high ground until it jumped into the creek. Hearing it walking in the water, and then that grunt when it landed on the bank traumatized me. It sounded like a tree fell when it landed. I served in the Air Force and went into some crazy places. I became an avid sportsman and always did a lot of fishing and hunting. I've walked up on rattlesnakes, bears, moose, and lots of other things that will scare you to death, but I have never had anything scare me and traumatize me like that experience did. Even now when I think about it the hair stands up on my arms. I've sat on this story for 47 years, and this is only the 2nd time I have shared it outside of my kids and my parents. My Dad did try to talk to James and Ronnie about what happened that day, but they wouldn't talk about it. All James would say is, "whatever your boy tells you happened that day is what happened." I've tried to go back to that location and just face my fears and walk into the woods there, but I just can't do it. To this day I am still traumatized by what happened that day."

"It Looked Like a Huge Spider Monkey"

Troup County, Georgia

The Myakka photos (2000)

This picture is only shown as an example and is not the property of the writer or the witness. This picture is copyrighted and belongs with the Myakka Skunk Ape Sightings report.

"I was driving from Mountville, headed back to Pine Mountain. I was driving a Toyota Four Runner and pulling an over-sized car trailer. I had borrowed the trailer the night before to pick-up a hot tub, and I had to have the trailer back to my brother-in-law the next morning because he needed to use it. There's a dirt road in Mountville that you can take, right where 'The Bargain Barn' used to be, called Chipley-Mountville Road. I turned there, and at the stop sign I turned right onto Dallas Mill Road. I drove about three miles, and I was approaching a creek close to where Frost School Road is on the right. It had rained heavily the night before, and the water was really rushing at the creek. I believe that's the only reason he did not hear me. I was only driving about five mph because it was a dirt road, and because of the trailer I was pulling and the hot tub. Before I got to the creek, I could see a bunch of vines moving on my left, so I started looking to my left as I crossed the creek. There's a metal pan that's grown into a tree right there where it happened. You can still see that pan in the tree. The creature was standing there on the creek bank pulling some type of vines. The vines looked like they were maybe honeysuckles or jasmine. I'm not really sure what type of vines, but the animal had a grip on them, and it was pulling them down. This animal's reach had to be at least 12 feet high, and he was standing down in a ravine. He looked to be about seven feet tall. This was not a very fat animal. He actually looked more slender and lean, and I could see gray and white hair down under his arms. He was black, and I could see black skin through the hairs because the sun was shining on him. It looked like he had balding patches on him. He looked at me, and I looked at him as I crossed the creek. He was only about 15 feet from me. As soon as he saw me, he immediately stopped moving and crouched down. I was kind of in shock as to what I had just seen, so it took me a few seconds to process it and stop. I tried to back up, but I couldn't because of the trailer I was pulling. I wasn't very good at backing a trailer back then, and I certainly was not going to get out of the vehicle. This creature had round black eyes that looked close together on the front of its head, but it also had a protruding nose like an orangutan. Its muzzle area was kind of tan looking, but it also looked like it had ears that were kind of flopped over. Now that I think about it, that could have just been matted hair because the creature was matted all over. I told my brother about it, and he told me I probably saw a bear. I did not see a bear that morning. This creature had shoulders, really long arms that were about the same length as his legs, and he had hands. I could see its black hands, and I could see the knuckles of its fingers. This thing had black hair all over it, with white and grey hair under its arms. The hairs hanging off the back of its arms were longer than the body hair. The best way I can describe it is that it looked like a huge spider monkey. This was definitely some kind of a primate that I saw. If it had a tail, I did not see one. I went back several times to see if I could see it again. I bought a camera, and I would purposely drive through there often. I even took my kids with me a few times, but we never saw anything else. I'm certain he just didn't hear me driving that morning because the water was rushing so hard from the rain the night before. I immediately started looking up stuff on the internet trying to figure out what it was, and the closest thing I have ever found is a skunk ape."

Eyewitness Report of Danny Skipper
Season-Spring 2017
Time: 7:00 a.m.
Report taken 10/25/2022

How Does a 1200 Pound Dead Cow Just Disappear?

Troup County. Georgia
Fall, 2012

"In 2012, I leased a pasture out Hwy 27 going towards Franklin, and I had a bunch of cows on it. The property was just before you got to Potato Creek. The property beside it had a huge hunting club on it, and on the other side was the Corp of Engineer property which is thousands of acres. The Chattahoochee River was only about a mile straight through the woods, and there was a creek that came all the way through the property and flowed all the way to the Chatta-hoochee.

One of the hunters from the club next door shot one of my cows, and I raised a big stink about it. I took my tractor and hauled the dead cow all the way to the back of the property and dropped it in a run-off ditch. I figured the coyotes, buzzards, and other animals would take care of it. I went back just a few days later and my son said he wanted to see the dead cow. Yes, I know it sounds morbid, but I drove him back there to see it and that 1200 lb. cow was nowhere to be found. I mean it just disappeared. There were no signs that anything had been eating on it. There were no drag marks, bones, blood, hair, nothing. It was just gone. I have no idea how a 1200 lb. cow can vanish just like that, but that one did.

After looking for that cow, I decided I better go check on my other cows and their calves. The cows were way down in the lower pasture next to the back gate that opened onto the Corps of Engineers' property. The creek flowed under the fence just a few feet from the gate. I was making sure the calves were doing ok and was focused on that until my son asked me if I heard that noise. I didn't hear anything then, but a few minutes later we heard a loud knock way down the creek. I could see that the cows had started moving towards the front pasture. It was quiet for a few minutes, so I whistled. Then it was quiet again and then it knocked again, but this time I could tell it was closer. I whistled again, then it knocked again, but this time it was really close. I grabbed my son up and we headed back to the truck which was at the barn in the middle pasture. We were completely exposed and a long way from the truck, and my hand never left the grip of the pistol I had on my side. I was watching our backs the whole time, and I wasn't going to stick around and find out what it was.

I will tell you something else that happened that makes the cow story even crazier. A few months after that happened, I got a call from my cousin. He had llamas not too far from there, and back then he was just learning about llamas. He didn't know you couldn't put two males together or they would fight to the death, and he ended up with a dead llama. He called me and told me what happened, and he asked me to bring my tractor over the next morning to help move the llama. Well, when I got over there with my tractor, we went down to where the llama was, but it was gone. This was about a 300 lb. llama. Again, there were no drag marks, no hair, no tracks, nothing. There was a bloody spot where it had been laying, but that was all. His pasture is surrounded by a five-strand barbed wire fence, and there wasn't anything even in the fence wire. I mean, you know how wooly a llama is, if something had dragged it off, it would have had to go through that fence and there would have been some hair in that wire. It looked like something just scooped it up and carried it away."

The following is a written report that was sent to me from the witness. I did not write the report, but I have been given permission to include his encounter story in this book.

"My Encounter: Near Amicalola River March 1974": Written and Submitted by My Friend Rick

"As an elementary school student in 1971 I saw Legend of Boggy Creek and I later read Peter Byrne's little paperback book on BF. The North GA mountains, especially the Appalachians, are rich with legends and strange stories about BOOGERS. Parents and adults would say "Don't be out at night, that's when the Booger Bears come out". Or "Don't go there, the Boogers will get you". And the most common term was "Booger Bear". The problem was, nobody would ever tell you what a Booger was or how it looked, so we thought it was only a scary story. In the Spring of 1973, a story circulated that a Game Warden went missing overnight and was found on a rural road walking the next morning by a farmer. He was exhausted and confused with his clothes torn and couldn't really remember what had happened. It was later said that he claimed to have seen a tall hairy creature with a big head and face like a Bull. This story was buzzing for about two weeks and suddenly all the talk of it went quiet. We think he either quit, or the State relocated him.

It was March of 1974, and I was 15. I didn't drink or smoke anything. I was a straight arrow football player and not the type to tell stories. About 8:00 p.m. I was riding in a car with 3 other guys, and the driver was about a year older than us. We were spot lighting Deer (Illegal) but not for the purpose of shooting one. Just checking them out. We were going down an old road that was barely paved and full of potholes. As we rolled along at about 10-15 MPH, we spotted a Buck and two Doe's up on a chest high red clay bank with bushes and overgrowth partially blocking our view. This was at a 4-Way crossroads where a very narrow dirt/gravel road led off to the right into a completely deserted forest with no houses. On the left was another dirt/gravel road with an old church on the corner. Further down that road were a couple of farms. A river runs down one side that is fed by Amicalola Falls which is located at the head of the Appalachian Trail. Ironically, there is an area of the river known as the Devil's Elbow where Moonshiners, car thieves, pot growers and hunters were alleged to have gone missing over the years. This is the same area where the Game Warden went missing.

I was in the passenger rear seat and couldn't really see the deer. We stopped and the guy in front of me got out with a spotlight, (an old D Cell) and shined the deer. It was apparent they had been running and were tired because they didn't haul ass when we lit them up. About 3 or 4 seconds after exiting the back seat I heard a crack/pop 45 degrees to my right in the forest toward the narrow road. My friend who was sitting next to me heard it and said, "Oh shit I bet that's a Game Warden", I said that's one noisy Game Warden. He then began urging the driver to get us out of there. About that time came more noise like something large moving through the woods. I instantly thought "Bear" because a 500 pounder was killed in our area, but bears are known to be quiet when walking. So, I start saying let's go and the hair starts standing up on my arms and neck and I began to feel sick with fear. About that time, approximately 75 or 80 feet to my right at a 15-20-degree angle, I watched a large Hulking figure cross that road from bank to bank in three forward-leaning large steps while swinging its arms. From the sound it was making it appeared to be approaching the deer, and at that moment they bolted out of there like shot from a cannon.

I was frozen with fear, and it seems like time has slowed down. My friend to the left says "What the Hell was that? And now we are both saying let's go, let's go, and we have one foot in the car. Then, as I look up on top of the embankment, I see the outline of a figure move slowly to get behind a tree about 60 feet away. Its face/head was obscured by the tree and limbs. My friend with the spotlight starts slowly getting in the car while me and the other dude dive in the back seat. At this time, my older and more stubborn friend pulls out a .22 caliber pistol and says, "Who are you? talk to me or I will shoot". Now we are screaming let's go as he again says, "Tell me who you are, or I will shoot". My friend in front of me still has the light pointed out over the door even though he is now back in the car. At that instant we hear bang, bang as the driver shoots up in the air. He immediately throws the pistol in the car and jumps in as we spin out of there sideways. Now I am shaking all over so badly that my feet are actually tapping and everybody, but the driver is talking at once. I don't remember who asked first, I think the guy in front, they got a better look, but he said, "What did ya see?" The driver is silent as we drove until we found a closed gas station and pulled in. Our driver got out and leaned over as if he would vomit. He then went to the drink machine and got a coke. He drank a little but still wouldn't talk.

So now my friend is driving us all home and it's almost 10:00 p.m. and we are planning to go back the next day to look around in daylight. We also agree to only tell our families minus the part about the gunfire of course. After we dropped off my friend in the back we headed to my house. My friend in front says to the driver, "Hey man, what did you see"? Nothing but silence until we get to my house where my friend in front says, "You saw its face didn't you"? He very quietly said "Umm". I sat there for a minute waiting for more, but it was obvious that he wasn't talking, and it was getting late on a school night. Then, of all things I had to get out and walk up the long path to the dark back side of my house which sat at the foot of a mountain. When I got inside my mom noticed that there was something wrong and her first question was "Has somebody been drinking"? Now that was all I needed. So, as I finally managed to tell my story, my mom replied "Huh, was probably the Devil". But my dad, who grew up on a farm only a few miles from this incident, sat silently looking at the TV. It was his older generation on both sides of the family who used the term BOOGER. Growing up on a farm he knew all too well about BOOGER stories and later said that he used to hear strange screaming sounds in the woods. on Panthers, but they were all hunted and killed off by the early 1900's. My Dad talked about walking from church one summer night with something following him. He said every time he stopped; it stopped. He said he pulled out his knife and walked home backwards for 1 1/2 miles until he got into the front porch light where "It" no longer followed him. I shared this story with a few people over the years but most laughed and ridiculed me, so I learned to shut my mouth.

So, the following day we all went back, and the driver was still not saying much. We get to the location and cannot find footprints but do find broken branches and impressions in the ground. Then we got to the tree where it's face was hidden. A prominent crooked limb stuck out and bent upward. I could stand flat footed and reach the limb with my arm almost extended. That put the creature at about 8" or more. We went back two times at night to look (Stupid & Heavily Armed) but found nothing thank God. About 3 months later I was in church and saw a girl that lived off the main road near there. I told her what happened, and a profoundly serious expression overtook her face. She informed me that it had run across the road in front of her one night while coming home from a football game. She also said that her uncle saw it coming out of his chicken house about a year prior. I sat there silently thinking oh God why have you allowed such things to exist?

In 1980 a new subdivision was being built near our encounter. A story started circulating that the first resident of this subdivision came home one night to find his back door broken down and his kitchen ransacked. Nothing stolen, just a destroyed kitchen. I didn't know the man but of all things he was related to my friend who drove the night of our encounter. Before church one morning some 6 years later, if he had heard about the break in and he simply said "Yes". I again asked did he see its face that night. He nodded yes and then looked away. The sight of "It" really scrambled his eggs and he didn't want to deal with it. As far as I know nothing ever came of the vandalized house incident as that story died quickly just like the Game Warden story. I later told my dad a story that my very peculiar aunt once told me at age 5 or 6. She and my uncle lived in a house on top of a big hill at the foot of a mountain about 5 miles from our incident. She claimed that while rocking on her front porch one night a large hairy man with a very ugly face came around the corner and stood motionless looking at her about 8 feet away. She said that she felt paralyzed with fear and could only cut her eyes to look at it. She was unable to call out to my uncle sitting in the living room behind only feet away. She claimed that she closed her eyes very tight and began praying, and in a few seconds, she opened her eyes, and it was gone. I remember her saying his face looked like it was hit by a hammer. I asked my dad if she was crazy to which he replied, "Folks thought so".

Later in life as a Criminal Investigator, long-time Drug Agent friend was temporarily put on detachment with the DEA. He told me about seeing these "Creatures" on a regular basis when staking out large "Grow Fields". He later questioned other agents about this, and they would nonchalantly say "Oh yeah, we see them all the time. He later learned that all video from stakeouts had to be immediately turned in so it could be scrubbed of these critters. Some areas around the GA FL line are so populated that personnel from state wildlife are assigned to the stakeouts along with occasional "Unknown Personnel" in black combat gear without uniform patches.

A Game Warden Buddy of mine would never discuss any of this until after he retired. He would only laugh it off and say, "Yeah I've heard all kinds of stuff". Much later after his retirement we reached an agreement where if I NEVER mentioned his name, I would ask questions and he would simply nod in the affirmative if I asked something he knew about. I was able to confirm that the "Big Black Bear" was often used for a Sasquatch sighting or incident. "Big Dogs", or "Black Dogs" are terms used for Dogman sightings. I was also able to confirm a story told me by a friend who moved into a new subdivision adjacent to a national park. He was one of the first residents in the early 90s and is an avid hunter. He called me and was obviously troubled. He said that lots of deer would congregate at night in his cul-de-sac and would hang out as people got into their cars to leave. He described seeing the "Biggest German Shepard or Wolf in his life" on the creek below his house. He also described loud coyote-like howls in the area that didn't sound right. My retired friend nodded in the affirmative as I presented the events.

As an Army Aviator in the 80's, I later learned about incidents surrounding the crash of an Army Cobra Helicopter in the mountains of North GA near an Army Ranger Camp. The Cobra had crashed at night and burned. Within about 5 or 6 hours six MPs arrived to secure the site until the next day when investigators arrived. The MPs set up tents and made a fire about 60 feet from the crash site. Sometime after midnight one MP heard a clanking noise and advanced to the site where he and another MP witnessed 3 large harry creatures pulling the pilot's bodies out of the wreckage. They opened fire over the heads of these creatures causing them to drop the bodies and flee. Not the behavior of friendly forest dwellers huh? I also later learned of a massive "Troop Exercise" out of Fort Campbell, KY where a large creature was hunted down and killed next to Land Between the Lakes. Whatever it was, it required a Deuce and a Half with a winch to pull its body up onto a ridge where a Chinook with a cargo net could carry it away.

Okay Angie, I hope that wasn't too boring. I just wonder how many people from my area have even better stories but won't come forward for fear of ridicule.

Sincerely, Rick"

Greg's Encounter Story

"I was hauling wood chips to a mill called West Rock in Maxville, Florida. I was about ten miles south of Baldwin off 219 headed towards Ocala. The mill was about four miles down this little narrow asphalt road. That road had several speed bumps, and you had to drive slowly over them. I was easing over the first speed bump when I watched a deer come out of the woods. The deer just walked like it was not in any hurry, it stopped for a second and looked at me, then just walked on across the road. Then when I got to the second speed bump, I saw another deer come walking out of the woods going in the same direction as the other deer, but then I saw a guy literally walking right behind the deer. I was so confused for a minute. It looked like the guy had on a Ghillie suit. The guy looked very ragged and looked like he had on very dirty green camo or something. I did not see any facial features because the guy was looking down the whole time. He did look bulky, maybe 250-300 pounds and about six feet tall. He didn't seem to have a neck, and his arms were kind of long and funny looking. Like I said, it looked like he had on some kind of hunting suit with long veils hanging off. The deer looked like she wasn't paying any attention to what the guy behind her was doing. I was trying to figure out how a hunter was able to get that close to a deer, and it was all just very confusing. They all just crossed the road and went into the woods on the other side. I didn't tell anyone what I saw, but one day me and a buddy were talking, and he told me something that happened to him. He said that a couple of years prior he was waiting to get his truck loaded, so he pulled his truck over to take a nap. It was about 3am, and he was approximately four or five miles away from where my incident happened. He said something started shaking his truck really hard and he raised up and saw it. He said whatever it was, looked him in the eyes because it was standing at his window. He said it jumped off the truck and ran into the woods."

Unfortunately, I was never able to get a better description of the creature the friend saw.

Possible Dogman Sighting Near Statesboro, Georgia

In August of 2020, a mother and daughter worked a weekend expo in Greensboro, Georgia. They finished the last night of the expo at about 10:30 p.m., then loaded all their merchandise into a 16ft box trailer, and headed back to the daughter's home in Statesboro, Georgia. It was sometime after midnight on Hwy 80, and near a little town known as "Hopeulikit." They recall the moon was bright that night because they were seeing a lot of deer. They were using the light of the moon to help watch for the deer and trying to avoid an accident. The daughter was driving and stated she had just looked at her GPS. She noticed they were only 15 minutes from home, and when she looked back to the road, she saw movement in the median. This was a four-lane divided highway with a grassy median. She started to brake preparing for a deer to possibly bolt in front of the truck. Both women could see something coming out of the median to cross the road, and both assumed it was a deer. Both women state they witnessed something on four legs come up out of the median, and transition onto two legs as it crossed the road in front of them just a few feet away. They claim the creature crossed the road within just a few steps as it was transitioning onto two legs. They describe the rear legs as resembling a dog, and that the creature was dark in color. They were unable to determine the exact color, but they believe dark gray or black. This happened very close to a home which had a yard light near the garage. They were able to watch the creature run through the yard and into the wood line near the house. They estimate the creature was approximately seven feet tall because it was taller than the road sign it ran behind. They describe the shoulders being wide, with long arms and long fingers and moving in a very unnatural way. Neither woman remembers the creature having a tail, but insists the head and ears looked like a German Shepherd. At that moment, both women could only describe it as a werewolf. They had traveled approximately 40 feet after seeing the creature, and something hit the side of the trailer they were pulling with enough force to shake the trailer and the Tahoe. They continued the drive home without stopping because they were too afraid to stop and check the trailer. Both women explain they have no idea what this creature was, but they both feel it was something evil and possibly demonic. They were both crying inconsolably after the sighting, and the daughter quickly sketched what they saw once they arrived home. I will include the sketch with this report.

This report is taken from an interview we did on the podcast five months ago titled, "Georgia Family Has Roadside Encounter." I found this family to be of good character and credible witnesses. If you would like to hear the interview for yourself, you can find the interview on our YouTube Channel, "The Sasquatch Encounter Brigade." You can also find us on several podcast platforms including Spotify, iHeart, Pod Bean and more.

Report taken June 27, 2024

"Daddy, Get in the Truck!"

Milner, Georgia

A family of four (husband, wife, 9-year-old daughter, 11-year-old son) had dinner in Griffin, Georgia on a Friday night one early fall evening in 2002. After dinner they decided to take their favorite backroads home which was a common thing for them to do. The wife states they would frequently take Hwy 19/41 towards Barnesville, then turn onto Five Points Road, and drive home through Pike County. They were in Milner, Georgia and her husband needed to pull over to use the restroom. He pulled his truck to the side of the road where he could see cars coming from either direction. He parked the truck with the lights still on, then walked behind his truck to relieve himself. The wife states that out of habit she rolled her window down just to listen out, and she could see the top part of her husband above the tailgate in her mirror. It was early fall, and the leaves had started to change but had not fallen from the trees yet. The kudzu was still green. The temp was about 50-60 degrees, and she was looking around at the leaves down the embankment into the tree line when there was movement in the bushes that caught her attention. The kudzu was in front of all the trees. She stated she then realized she was looking into the face of a creature that was within 30 yards of their vehicle. She states, "I saw its hand go up on the tree and I could see the entire fingers, the arm, the shoulder, and the full head. It literally put its hand up and pushed itself kind of around the tree peeking to see what was going on." She states she felt like her heart hit her stomach and all she could say was "*****, get in the truck. *****, get in the truck" to her husband. It was then the son and daughter also saw the creature and began to start crying and screaming, "Daddy, get in the truck." The witness states the creature appeared to be watching her husband, but her husband did not see the creature. She states the creature looked like it took one step backwards and was gone from sight.

Description of the creature from all three witnesses -skin texture of silverback gorilla. The nose was not flat, but it had big nostrils. Hair that came down to the eyebrow line and around the chin. Could make out its lips and eyes. The eyes were very human-like but dark. The skin texture on the fingers was very leathery and an ash grey color. They could see the bend of the fingers and the nails. It had hair that came down on top of the hand, but not really on the fingers. Its hand was human-like but huge. Its hair appeared to be four-to-five inches long over its body. Dark brown hair, but the tips seemed to be reddish as if the sun had bleached it out a bit. The three witnesses saw the face, the right shoulder, right arm, right hand, and part of the chest. They report the body was very muscular and they did not see a conical shape to the head. Witnesses stated the area was very heavily wooded and they stopped close to a creek. They speculated the creature was on the creek and may have been curious when they stopped on the side of the road.

This family has asked to remain anonymous. I interviewed this family and the wife twice. Her story never changed, and I find this family to be of reliable character. They are all business professionals in a neighboring city. The children are now grown, and they both state they can still vividly remember what they saw as children that night with their mother.

Report taken January 8, 2023

I Told the Lord, "I Don't Know What it Was, but I Know What I Saw, and I Know You Created It."

I met a man named Mr. Crane in the park today in Williamson, Ga. We had a 12:30 p.m. appointment and he was already there when I arrived. We have a mutual friend named Mr. Bobby Bunn, and Mr. Bunn helped arrange our meeting. Mr. Bunn had already told me what a fine Christian man Mr. Crane was, and I found his opinion of Mr. Crane to be very accurate. We ended up talking about the Lord almost as much as we talked about Bigfoot. That's one of the reasons I love this subject matter so much. My research of Bigfoot often takes me back to the Bible to study more about creation, angels, demons, giants, and all sorts of other very interesting stuff.

The very first thing he said to me after we introduced ourselves was, "I told the Lord, I don't know what it was, but I know what I saw, and I know you created it." Before he told his encounter story, I told him I wanted to know more about him first. He explained he was 84 years old and had retired from the United States Postal Service several years ago. Before his career began at the post office, he had served in the United States Navy as well. I did not ask him, but I got the impression he had lived around Spalding/Pike County all his life. He told me a little about his family and we talked about our faith in Jesus Christ for a few minutes, then he dove right in telling me what he witnessed that day. The following is his story.

"Well, this happened about 50 years ago. It would have been around November and sometime in the 70s. My father-in-law bought a farm off Jackson Road, just before Wallace Road. Back then it was called 'Crapo Farm', but it's over-grown now. If you know where the Dollar General Ware-house is in Jackson, this would be on the opposite side of the dirt road. The farm was over 200 acres and back then I was big into hunting and fishing. He would let me hunt there sometimes, and on this particular day I had taken my father with me.

We went through a cattle gate on the road and drove across the field until we reached the tree line. It was a wooded hill-side overlooking a creek. My father was going to hunt from the ground, and I had built myself a deer stand about 50 yards into the woods. I was in my deer stand and my father was sitting about 100 yards from me. We had been there for about 45 minutes I guess, when I heard something that sounded like leaves rustling. I clicked my safety off expecting to see a deer, but I didn't see a deer. I kept hearing the leaves rustling and that's when I saw a creature about four-to-five feet tall standing under a big oak tree. Then I heard something that sounded like a moan coming from the creek and there was another creature, but this one was about 7-8 feet tall. The larger creature walked to the smaller creature, and then it let out another softer sounding moan and took the smaller creature's hand. I was in shock. They walked away from me, and toward the part of the creek that goes under I-75 now. I watched them until they were out of sight. I lowered my gun and got out of that stand as fast as I could. When I got to my father, he asked me what was wrong because my hair was standing straight up, he said. I told him what I had seen, and we left.

I called my brother-in-law, whose father-in-law was a sheriff's deputy, and we went back the next morning. Where the small one had been, the whole area under that tree was bare, just like someone had cleared all the leaves out from under it. I guess that was the leaf rustling sound I kept hearing. We went down to the creek and found a footprint in a soft mossy area. The print was probably 12-14 inches long.

Now, this part is hearsay, but I was told his father-in-law called the game warden and they went back and took a plaster cast of that print. I was told they found 'more evidence', but I was never told what it was, and I never heard anything else after that."

I thought this was an amazing encounter to witness, especially the interaction between the adult and its young. I asked Mr. Crane more questions and learned a few more details. He said he never saw the face because the creatures were downhill from him. He was about 15 feet high in his deer stand, and the stand was uphill from the creatures. He said they were both the same color, with very dark brown hair that was at least 4-5 inches long. He said he didn't know for sure, but he just felt like the adult was a female because of the motherly behaviors towards the juvenile. He said they just looked like a mother and a child holding hands as they walked off together. He doesn't feel like the creatures ever knew he was there.

I asked him about his father-in-law and what his impression was of the event. He said his father-in-law wasn't a very talkative man anyway, and he never really said much more about it. He said his father-in-law lived on the property, and if he had any experience with the creatures he never talked about it, but he did sell that property after that.

Mr. Crane said he stopped hunting that day, except for the very few times he went hunting with his brother in a different location, and he eventually stopped completely. He has told his story a few times throughout his life, and it doesn't bother him at all if someone doesn't believe him. He says he knows for sure what he witnessed that day. He says he stands firm in his Christian faith and whatever it was, it was something God created, so he decided to just leave it at that and not worry about what others think.

Mr. Crane also mentioned he had heard a rumor about a Bigfoot sighting years ago on the dam at the Griffin Reservoir, so if anyone has any leads on this sighting, please let me know!!

3/29/2025

"We Walked Back to the Truck in Silence, and My Dad Never Hunted Again"

"My name is Tracy Hall, and I know for certain Bigfoot is real. I wasn't really a believer until I saw one for myself. It was October of 1987, my dad and I were deer hunting in Forsyth County, Georgia. We arrived at the orchard on our property before daylight that day, and as soon as we stepped out of the vehicle we were hit with an overwhelming smell of skunk, septic tank, and rotted meat. The smell was so strong we looked around for about ten minutes trying to find the source of the smell but never found anything.

We walked about 300 yards to my dad's blind that he had previously sat on top of the root ball of a fallen tree. James Creek was about 60 yards from his blind, and my tree stand was across James Creek, and about another 150 yards away with a big hill between us. I continued to my stand and crossed James Creek which was about eight feet wide and ankle deep. I climbed into my stand which was about ten feet high. About 25 yards away was another creek and a dirt bike trail the deer also used.

I had only been in my stand for about 30 seconds when I heard heavy footsteps walking from the direction of the motorcycle trail. It was still rather dark, and I could barely see. I asked myself 'who would be walking through here without a flashlight?' Then I thought it may be a cow, but the footsteps sounded bipedal, so I was confused. After another 30 seconds or so, I could see movement coming down the trail. It was about 50 yards away and it was still too dark to really see anything.

I raised my field glasses (provide better visibility in low-light conditions) to get a better look and immediately thought it was someone walking on stilts and was very confused. I raised the glasses again and saw matted fur under its arm pits. At this point the creature was only about 20 yards away and headed straight towards me. There was a small ditch between me and the creature, and when he stepped over that ditch, I realized what I was looking at.

I had never believed in the existence of Bigfoot before then. I had read about it a few times but really thought there was no way those things were real. It never broke stride and continued towards me. When it was only 12-15 feet from me when it crossed under my stand. I could have touched it with the barrel of my gun because this creature was about nine feet tall. It looked like a brahma bull on two legs, and looked as if it was about four feet thick.

I was dumbfounded and felt like I was dreaming. I couldn't see any facial features and saw more of a silhouette, but I could tell its head was as big as a five-gallon bucket. It never looked in my direction and it never occurred to me to shoot it, and it was headed in the same direction I had come in from. I kept watching it through my field glasses and watched it step over a four-foot drainage ditch like it was nothing. After a few seconds I could only see it from the waist up, but I could still see the massive muscling in its back and shoulders.

I lost sight of it for a few seconds but then saw it again and realized it was headed straight towards my dad. I heard a huge splash and was able to watch it for about another 20 seconds as it crossed over the hill that was between me and my dad. I had to calm down for a minute and figure out a plan. Then it occurred to me that my dad may have a heart attack if he sees this thing, and I began to panic. I had no choice but to head in that same direction to my dad.

Soon as I could see the orange of my dad's vest I began to whistle, and he wasn't moving. I began to really panic and kept whistling until he abruptly turned around and said, 'That's a good way to get shot.' He explained that I had been walking around in front of him a few minutes earlier and even making a loud splash when I fell in the creek.

I explained to him it wasn't me and walked to where he thought he saw me. I am 6'2" and weigh about 180 pounds. Dad became confused as to what he had witnessed. He said what he saw was 3-4 times larger than I was and a foot taller than my hand when I raised it as high as I could.

We decided to look around and see if we could find any tracks or see anything else. We walked down to the creek and found where the edge of the bank had collapsed into the creek. That was the loud splash we had heard. We found some large impressions and one large footprint at the creek where the bank had collapsed. We could see where it had crossed over. The footprint was extremely large, and I could place all four fingers in the big toe print.

We walked back to the truck in silence, and my dad never hunted again. He refused to talk about it. When asked, he would just say 'I don't want to talk about it' and walk away. Sometimes he would go into his bedroom and just close the door if the topic came up.

I never saw anything again, but in that same area there were some other strange occurrences. My uncle had a commercial hog farm, and he showed up to work early one morning to find the huge barn door was broken and a 350-400 pound sow was missing. Something had picked it up and carried it out of there because the gate was still latched. This was a commercial farm, with different levels, so if the hog had simply gotten out of its pen, it would have still been enclosed.

Also, there was a herd of cows killed one night. There was a write-up in the Forsyth County News. All the cows had been killed, and they all had holes in their necks as if all the blood had been drained."

"All Through These Years, it Still Lingers in My Mind."

In the spring of 2000, I met my friend Tara Kinsey. We are opposites in so many ways, but in a way that I cannot explain, our souls just connected. She had brought her son into the pediatric clinic I was working at, and I knew I wanted to be friends with her soon as we met. We quickly became friends because we shared a love for horses. We spent a few years riding together and sharing some deep conversations about everything under the sun.

I specifically remember her telling me about a "white Bigfoot" she saw as a kid. Now, when she told me this, I honestly thought she was probably just seeing things as a kid, especially since she was saying she saw a white one. I mean, there is no way I was going to believe an abominable snowman was in Georgia. I didn't think she was lying, I honestly just thought it was a case of mistaken identity by a kid and didn't think much more about it.

Years later, when I became interested in researching Bigfoot phenomena, I saw where others around the south have reported seeing white Bigfoot. There are numerous reports of "The Alabama White Thang" along with several others reported throughout the United States, including the southern states. I remembered Tara's story and knew that I was going to ask her about it eventually. She had moved away, and we lost touch for several years, but luckily, we reconnected through social media. One evening she sent me a message and asked if I had ever heard of anyone else seeing a light gray or even lighter colored Bigfoot around Blairsville, Ga.

I told her I had heard of numerous sightings of white or very light-colored Bigfoot and had been wanting to talk with her again about her sighting. I had always assumed the sighting was in Newnan, Georgia where she grew up, but it was in Blairsville, Georgia. She stated she stumbled across a DNR report of some sort about 10 years prior that mentioned a sighting of a light colored "bear", but the witnesses were adamant it was not a bear. She said she reached out to me because all through these years, it still lingered in her mind and out of all her friends I'm probably the only one that don't think she's crazy. I don't think she's crazy and her story hasn't changed in 25 years. This is her story:

"There were four or five of us kids, but I was the oldest. I was no older than ten years old, and the others were about six years old. Our families had gathered at my uncle's cabin in Blairsville, Ga. and us kids decided to go bike riding. We were just young kids and had stopped to play at a burned-down house on the side of the mountain. The only reason we could really see it was because the leaves had all fallen. We heard something coming down the ridge, and I thought it was the Easter Bunny because of its color, and it was upright. I know now it couldn't have been a bear either because it came all the way down the slope upright. It didn't come at us, it just continued walking at a fast pace and continued straight down the slope. The roadway was below, and it was bordered by more woods.

We were very scared, and the adults went looking for it after we told them what we all saw. The adults thought it was a bear, but bears don't walk upright for that long. It was tall because there was some distance between us, and it was big. I remember it being light colored, like light gray or whitish in color."

After further discussion with Tara, we determined the incident occurred around 1987 or 1988, and on or near Knights Way road, in Blairsville, Ga.

nine
the okefenokee report

This Entire Chapter is Dedicated to Our Friend Kevin Crawford.

Our friend Kevin passed away while I was writing this book. Him and his sweet wife Doris were so good to us while we visited. Kevin was passionate about his love of Bigfoot and the quest to discover the truth. He knows the truth now, and one day we all will. I wish he was here to read my first book. He would have loved being a part of it. He never really understood how much of a door he opened for me, just by reaching out to our group and helping with this trip that weekend. I am eternally grateful for his friendship and his enthusiasm.

This section contains the actual report as it was written, with only a few changes to make the report fit into this book.

Angie Williamson

The Okefenokee Swamp Report

A collection of reported sightings, encounters, and possible evidence within a 100 mile radius of Waycross, GA.

Artwork compliments of Mallorie Fountain

This report is based on our team's first trip into the swamp and surrounding areas in hopes of finding evidence of Sasquatch. We found a little more than we bargained for. With numerous eye-witness reports, we were invited to investigate this beautiful tranquil refuge by a local family. We enjoyed exploring some of the areas, and of course we seized the opportunity to get close to nature. We were able to meet with locals who shared stories of their encounters, and they allowed us to make official reports for our team's records. We met some great people that made us feel like family, and we made some good friends along the way.

The Okefenokee Swamp is one of the most beautiful and often overlooked places in Georgia. It is considered the headwaters of the St. Mary's and the Suwannee River, and with its unique ecosystem and isolation, it has become a sanctuary for wildlife, including approximately 13,000 alligators. The Okefenokee is home to an abundance of plant life, and to a variety of endangered species because it is one of the world's largest freshwater ecosystems. It wasn't until this investigation began that I learned how pure the swamp water is. A glass of the water looks like weak tea due to the tannic acid, but locals say they will challenge its purity and flavor against mountain spring water anywhere. The tannic acid from certain trees prohibits the growth of bacteria, and allows the water to stay fresh longer, even without refrigeration.

In addition to the abundant wildlife, the swamp is also a place of history, folklore, and mystery. The swamp's first inhabitants were Native Americans. They named the swamp "Okefenokee", which means "land of the trembling earth." The swamp is about 10,000 years old and covers approximately 700 square miles. During the Seminole Wars of the 19th century, a few Native Americans were able to avoid capture by hiding in the swamp.

Over time they were joined by escaped slaves and AWOL soldiers, and a community was formed. Their leader's name was "Billy Bowlegs", and this is who many believe Billy's Island is named after. Considering the history of Billy's Island, it is understandable why so many tales and legends are told regarding this island in the middle of a swamp.

The Okefenokee provided a lot of hunting and fishing for numerous tribes of Native Americans, with the last of the Seminoles being driven out of the swamp in 1838. The U.S.

Fish and Wildlife Service acquired the majority of the 400,000 acres of the swamp in 1937. While no hunting is allowed in the swamp currently, some fishing is still allowed.

Special Thanks:

Thank you to the locals for your wonderful Southern hospitality, and for sharing your beautiful land with us. A special thank you to Kevin Crawford for reaching out to us and helping with all aspects of the investigation, and to his sweetheart of a wife Doris, for all her hospitality and support. They were both instrumental in making connections with witnesses and helping us navigate areas to camp amongst many other things. We are looking forward to Part 2 and can hardly wait to return. Thank you, Steve Hester, for sharing your experiences, taking us to the location of your sighting, and sharing your wealth of knowledge about the area. Thank you, Barb Kramer for sharing your stories of the swamp, and all your help with locations and contacts.

Eyewitness Reports

Paul's 1st Encounter

Paul: Former military
Year: 1988
Season: Summer
Time: Approximately 10:00p.m.

Location: Hwy 40 between Folkston and Kingsland. Camden County.

Witness testimony: "I worked on base and lived in Folkston. After work sometimes, we would drive to a place in Kingsland to shoot pool, have a couple of beers, and then we would head back home. The way we would go had very little traffic, and there was a place about half-way that we would frequently stop at to relieve ourselves of the beers. That night I was driving and pulled over like we had done so many times before. Right when I pulled over my friend suddenly flopped down in the seat and started saying 'Man, you almost hit that guy.' I jumped out of my car to tell the person I almost hit that I was sorry, and that did not see them when I pulled over. My friend kept saying that it was a man dressed in black, and that I was so close to him that my friend saw his face. I was saying 'hey man, I didn't see you dressed all in black', but there was no one there.

We went ahead and relieved ourselves. I was at one end of the car, and he was at the other. The way we were facing was towards the tree line, and there was a wire cattle fence. While we were standing there the entire fence started shaking, and the wire was squeaking, and we could hear whatever it was blowing really loud. It was blowing and kind of snorting and grunting. We jumped back in the truck and left."

Paul's 2nd Encounter

Year: 1989
Season: Fall
Time: Approximately 9:00p.m.
Location: Charlton County on the Saint Mary's River. Old River Road.

Witness testimony: "There's a place there that goes down to the river where people like to swim, build bonfires, and hang out at night. When I first moved to this area, I was warned to watch out for the hermit that lives in a hollow tree, and it is very swampy on the west side of where the swimming area is. I don't really think there's anyone actually living in a hollow tree down there, but I always thought it was a cool story, especially after what happened.

I went there one night with my roommate, and we were just talking when we heard a dog howl way off in the distance and didn't think much of it. It almost sounded like it was running deer miles away, but then it started getting closer and louder. Within two minutes it was even louder and closer, and it no longer sounded like a dog. I sounded like a cross between a howl, a scream, and a growl. That's when we decided it wasn't a dog. Then it let out a literal guttural scream like I once heard on an episode of a Bigfoot show. We could tell it was coming our way, so we jumped into the car. When we turned on the headlights we could see the tree line, and we could see something running up and down the tree line grabbing trees and shaking them. Whatever it was, it stayed just inside the tree line, and it ran the distance of where the headlights hit the trees. I could just see the movement and the shaking of the trees, and we left.

I worked with a guy that lived close to that area. I asked him if he'd ever heard anything down there on Old River Road, and he said, 'oh, you've heard the howls'."

Kelly Herndon's Encounter

Year: Approximately 1982
Season: Fall
Time: 5:20 a.m.
Location: Surrency, Ga. In the Surrency Flat Woods Area. On a black water creek bed on a family-owned farm.

Witness Testimony: "I am 54 years old, and I grew up in Surrency, Ga. I grew up on a cattle farm, and I've been hunting and fishing all my life. We had pastureland, a lake, woods, and a creek bottom filled with Cypress trees and dark sandy soil. My mom used to lock us out of the house during the day when we were kids, and we'd stay outside playing and riding 3 wheelers, or an old army jeep on dirt roads all day long once we got a little older. I'm just telling you this so you will understand that I grew up outdoors and in nature. I also can tell you that I am an avid hunter and fisherman. I've had a lot of experience hunting and spending time in the woods. I have taken many trophy deer, and what happened to me that one morning was not a deer. We have never seen any signs of bears on the property, and we didn't have hogs there until about 5-10 years ago.

We were about 30 miles from the Okefenokee Swamp in an area known as 'The Flat Woods Area'. I went deer hunting that morning deep into the creek bottom with a climber stand. There was an old logging road that is now just a trail, and I went down that road about 100 yards to where I was going to hunt. It was about 5:00 a.m., and I climbed about 25 feet up the tree. Going in that early would give me time to get completely settled before daylight. I had used a flashlight to get to my location by pointing it directly onto the ground on my way in so as not to spook the deer. It was pitch black dark and there was no moon that morning. We would always locate our tree and just turn off the flashlight and leave it at the bottom of the tree because we wouldn't have a need for it in the tree, and then we could just grab it when we came back down. I laid the flashlight down and climbed the tree as quietly as possible just like I had been taught.

I had been sitting in the tree quietly for about 20 minutes waiting on the daylight, when I began to hear something coming from about 200 yards away. Whatever it was, it sounded like it was trying to step on and break everything it could. It was as if it was being loud on purpose. Like it wanted everything to know it was coming through. It kept coming in my direction and I could tell it was walking on 2 legs. I have been hunting since the age of 5, so I know for sure it was walking on 2 legs. I just couldn't get over how it was purposely breaking everything it could find to break. It was wet in the creek bottom, so there was no crunching of leaves. That's why the deer like to move around there because they can walk without making any noise. It just kept getting closer and closer, and when it was about 50 yards from me it stopped. There was dead silence. I was just sitting there listening. At this point I was telling myself this still had to be a deer because what else could it be. We had never seen a bear or any signs of bears on the property. I sat there for about 5 more minutes in total silence. There were no crickets, no frogs, no birds, nothing. Usually, the forest would have started to come alive at this point but there was only silence. Then, as if it could see me in the dark, it made a 90 degree turn and headed straight towards me. I could tell the limbs it was breaking were big. I listened to its gait...the walk, and I started freaking out.

At this point I had begun to think this must be a person, and I was thinking to myself, 'am I going to have to shoot this person?' As it was walking, I could tell it was big and knew it had to weigh at least 300 pounds, and I was trying to figure out how this person could see me. It walked directly under me, and I could hear its deep breathing. I could not see it, but I could tell by the sound of its breathing that it was looking straight up the tree at me. I could just hear its heavy deep breaths and I really did not know what to do. I was sitting there holding a major weapon, but I had been trained to know your target before shooting. It stood there for what seemed like 5 minutes, and then it just walked off...breaking everything it could find in its path. It was like it was just looking for limbs to step on and break.I could tell it was following the creek, and I believe now that it had smelled me.

I thought I was literally going to have a heart attack. I could hear my own heart beating. I waited until daylight, and I left that morning. It changed how I hunt. After that morning I always go in at gray light. I have never walked into the woods an hour before daylight since, and I always carry my flashlight up the tree with me now."

Photo of location of encounter compliments of
Kelly Herndon

Ashleigh's Sighting

Year: Approximately 2014
Season: Late fall
Time: Approximately 7:30a.m.
Location: Barnard Road. Bryant County. Richmond Hill,
Ga. The area is close to the middle school and tree farm.

"My encounter was back in approximately 2014. It was around the holidays, and it was about 7:30a.m. I was on the bus, and we had pulled down a side road to pick up a student. Where we turned back onto the main road, there was a blue trailer type home and a tree that was about 50-60 feet tall. I was just listening to music and looking out the bus window when I saw it. It looked like a baby bigfoot. It was jumping around and swinging in the top of the tree from branch to branch. It was hanging on by one of its arms with its other arm curled around itself. As the bus drove past it, the little thing jumped straight down to the ground from the top of the tree, and then it darted back into the woods. The little creature wasn't little in the definition sense of the word. It was probably the size of a 9-10 yr. old child that was well fed and well built. This was all in Bryant County, Richmond Hill area towards the middle school and the tree farm that's next to it. It was on Barnard Road, off Harris Trail Road."

Angie Williamson

Anonymous Eyewitness Encounter

Year: Approximately 2008
Season: Winter
Time: Approximately 11:30 p.m.
Location: Close to the auction house, 4th Street Extension, Alma, Bacon County.

Witness testimony submitted via messenger: "I live in Alma, but I have seen a few strange things around the old Dixie School, and the 4th Street Extension area in Bacon County. One night, probably 14 years ago, I was driving home and looked away from the road to adjust the heat in my car. When I looked back up there was a tall black thing standing right next to the driver's side window. It looked feathery, but it also felt like time slowed down, and when I stopped and turned around it was gone. I've also seen odd looking lights in the sky around here, including one that was just an odd-looking light at first glance, but it actually split apart into two separate lights."

I did advise the witness of my theory of "time slowing down". I believe the witness may have been hit with infrasound. Many researchers believe Sasquatch has the ability to incapacitate its prey with infrasound, and the creature may also use it as a defense mechanism. I also advised that the "feathery" look could have just been matted hair, but who knows what it could have actually been.

PICTURES SUBMITTED BY LOCALS

Following photos are courtesy of Cynthia Wade and taken in Ralph E. Simmons State Park Forest on the St. Mary's River. Horseback not required but suggested.

Possible den. Photos compliments of Cynthia Wade

Possible marker aka asterisk. Photo compliments of Cynthia Wade

Possible marker aka asterisk and possible trees
pushed over to block access. Photo
compliments of Cynthia Wade

Photo courtesy of Cynthia Wade. Possible marker located in Ralph E. Simmons State Park Forest on the St. Mary's River. Horseback not required but suggested.

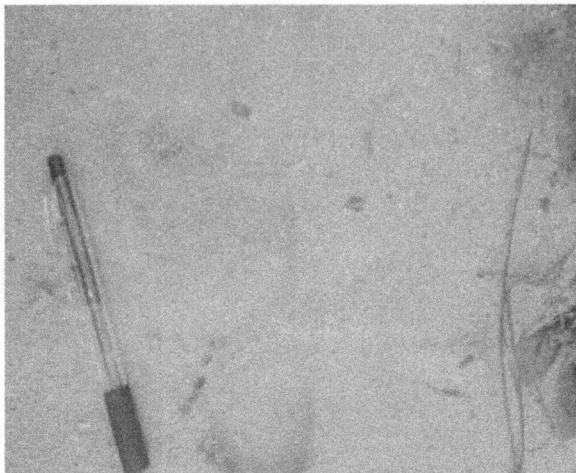

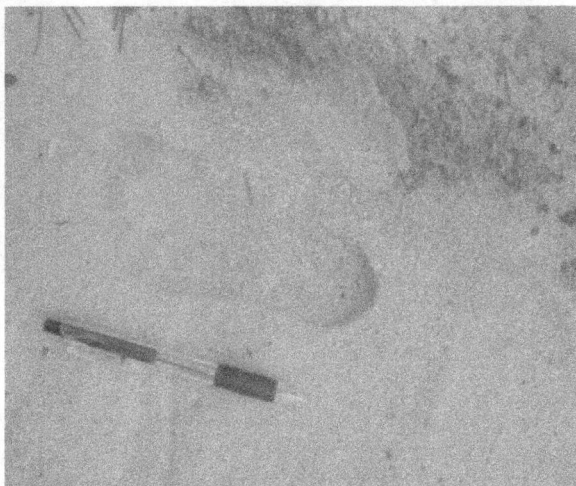

Possible right and left infant Sasquatch
footprints compliments of Kevin Crawford.
Pictures taken on the roadway in an isolated
area near the Satilla River. No other tracks
accompanied these small tracks, and Kevin
reports that no infant should be walking in
the area he found the tracks.

LOCALS TELL OF THEIR ENCOUNTERS

Steve Hester's Story

"I have a great friend that I went to school with, and one night I stayed at her house so I could go deer hunting on her property early the next morning. I would say it was about 2016, and the property is in the Bickley Community just off Old Nichols' Highway. I got into the woods that morning at about 5am., and I climbed into my stand about an hour before daylight. I wasn't in the stand for long, when I heard something that sounded like someone picked up a log and hit it against a tree. I had no doubt when I heard the sound what it was. I quickly climbed down from my stand, and then it occurred to me that he would not have hit the tree like that unless he knew I was there, so I went right back up. I waited until daylight to come back down. The sound I heard that day was unreal, and I never returned to that location again. As a matter of fact, I quit hunting that day and I have not hunted since. What makes this story so crazy is what happened next.

About two years later I was driving on Old Nichols' Highway, and I was driving back from Nichols where I had visited a friend. It was wintertime and it was foggy that night. At about 9:00 p.m. I got close to the road where I had originally heard that sound, and I saw a pair of great big red eyes. It had a lot of smaller eyes behind it, and I could tell the smaller eyes were deer in the back of the field. As I was approaching, it ran across the road in front of me on two legs. It ran faster than any deer I have ever seen. It passed in front of a road sign that was about 9.5 feet tall, and its head was just below the road sign. It was a grayish color, and it was huge. At first, I thought my eyes were playing tricks on me, and then I realized I was almost to the location where I had originally heard the log being beaten against a tree. I called my friend that still lived there, and I told her what I had just witnessed. The next day we went looking for tracks, and we found one in the soybean field that was 17.5 inches long. I took pictures with my cell phone, but that phone has since crashed, and I've been trying to find someone that can access those pictures. I also believe I heard one on the Satilla River one day. I went to look at a cabin off Central Avenue that I was interested in buying. As soon as I stepped out of the vehicle, I heard it. It sounded like it was about a mile away, but it was so long winded and powerful there was no mistaking what it was."

Homer Thornton's Story

"I have had two encounters, and it was in the fall the year I had my first encounter. I believe it was around September 2012. Me and a group of buddies were doing some night fishing. We were in Waycross on the 121 extension, and we were walking through an area that had recently been clear cut. There was one small area of scrub oaks that had been left uncut. As we were walking by that little patch of oaks, we all saw some movement and shined our lights to see what it was. What we saw was something large and black. We thought it was a bear that was pacing back and forth. We could see red eyeshine, and it had forward-facing eyes. It never took its eyes off us, and we felt threatened because of the way it was acting. Looking back now, I imagine it probably wasn't pacing. It was probably rocking back and forth because its eyes never turned at all. I thought we were about to be attacked by an angry black bear, so I shot it. When I shot it, it let out the most horrible growl I have ever heard, and it kept standing there growling. I knew then that I had only made it mad, and it was not a bear we were dealing with. It wasn't until I shot it two more times with my 30.06 that it disappeared. I grew up in the Okefenokee, and I have been hunting and fishing all my life. I could tell by the sound that I hit the creature all three times I shot. We went back the next day to see if we could find anything. We did not find anything at all. It was so weird that there was not even a drop of blood that we could find. We looked all around the area and could not find any blood, hair, or anything."

"My second encounter happened several years later in Jesup, Ga. It was early Spring 2016. My cousin, myself, and a buddy were fishing on the Altamaha River. We were on a sandbar fishing for about 12 hours. We got there about 1:00 p.m. that day and packed up to leave about 1:00 a.m. We had about a half of a mile hike back to the vehicles. We walked down the sandbar about 400 yards, and we were about 20 yards into the woods when my cousin turned around and said, 'I just heard someone call my name in Homer's voice'.

We all shined our lights around and didn't see anything. We walked about another 100 yards, and it did it again except this time it called my name in my cousin's voice. We thought it was another one of our buddies messing with us, so I yelled for him to come out because we were all armed. Soon as I yelled for our buddy to come out, it let out that same horrible growl with the same scary emotions I heard four years prior. It must have watched us and learned how to mimic our voices and our names. We were there about 12 hours, so there's no telling how long it had been watching us that day."

Lamar E's Story

"It was summer of 1998, when I was about ten years old, that I saw Bigfoot behind Martin's Mobile Homes in Blackshear. I was with my friend, who passed away in 2013. We were fishing in a pond on Eli Manning Circle, off Highway 84. We heard some noise from across the pond that sounded like an animal moving through the woods. Then, suddenly there he stood. He stood on two feet with black hair that looked like a bear. He had to have been about eight feet tall or taller. He looked at us for about 10-15 seconds and that felt like an hour. Then, suddenly, he jumped into the pond feet first, and we took off running. We left our fishing poles and everything behind. We ran all the way back to my house which was about two miles away. We told our parents, but they didn't believe us and laughed us off. We didn't sleep at all that night and just kept staring out the window afraid. I have not been back there since."

John Pearson's Story

"I grew up in Waycross, Georgia, and in approximately 1988 my cousin and I were spending the night at our grandparent's house on Albany Ave, in Waycross. We decided to camp for the night in our Mee-Maw's backyard in a four-person tent. I was about eight years old, and my cousin was about ten years old. I remember it was in the fall, and the only light we had was from the yard light.

We grew up hearing stories about wood boogers, the swampland, and it was also common for a six-to-eight-foot gator to be in the yard. We were quite brave and not really scared of much because we were used to the stories and the gators, but I am certain we had a sasquatch walk around our tent that night. We were already asleep when we woke up to the sounds of someone walking around the tent. The yard light cast a shadow on the tent from the creature, and we could tell from the shadow that it was huge. The shadow was massive, and we could hear it breathing as it was walking around the tent. It finally wandered back into the woods towards the small pond behind their house and didn't bother us anymore that night.

The next morning, we told the adults what happened, and my Pa said that we could not camp anymore. The adults didn't really say much, but we could tell they were acting weird. Looking

back on it now, I guess they didn't really want to scare us kids too badly, but they knew what had probably walked around the tent that night and knew it wasn't safe for us to camp like that again".

Kevin Crawford's Story

"It was about 1968, and I was about five years old. My daddy was on leave from Germany, and we would be moving to California soon where he would be stationed. We were staying at my grandmother's house in Blackshear just temporarily, and it was kind of a tradition that Daddy would take us to the Okefenokee Swamp Park before we would move to a new place. We would be leaving for California the next day, so that day my daddy was taking us to the park. We turned off U.S. 1 and onto Highway 177. It was about 10 a.m. and we were about a mile in. My daddy noticed it first and was telling Mama, 'That's not a bear. A bear can't walk that far on his hind legs.' That got my interest, so I popped my head up from the backseat to see what they were talking about. It was coming from the left side knee-deep in the swamp. It walked 40-50 feet in the swamp on two legs, and then up the embankment on two legs. It stopped and turned and looked at us, and Daddy stopped the car about 40 yards away. It turned back and kept walking straight off the road into the swamp on the other side. I remember it was huge and covered in black hair. I remember it being very tall. I believe it was about nine feet tall.

My 2nd sighting happened about 4 years ago. Doris had a candle show the next day and we were up late packing and getting ready. It was about 2:30a.m. and Doris wanted to smoke, so we went out to sit in our rocking chairs on the front porch. It was raining that night, and I looked up and saw this thing walking down the road. It was way skinnier than the other one, and at first I thought it was a person. I even told Doris, 'what's this idiot doing walking down the road in the rain this time of morning.' This one was solid brown looking and looked like it was about seven feet tall. I watched it walk until my truck blocked my view and then I never saw it again. It did turn and look at us, so I don't know if it stayed behind my truck until we went in, or if it turned and went out across the field."

Our Story

Seems as though weird encounters have occurred in or around the Okefenokee Swamp for centuries. Numerous reported sightings of UFOs, swamp gas, floating lights, ghostly encounters, swamp hags, and finally...the swamp boogers. Skunk Ape, Pig Man, Wood Booger, or plain ol' Bigfoot are just a few of the names of this mysterious creature that brought our team to the beautiful Okefenokee Swamp to investigate for ourselves. I started this trip as a believer, and on March 5, 2022, at approximately 10:15p.m. I became a "knower".

On Friday night, March 4, 2022, myself, Scott Deforest, John Pearson and his wife April Pearson drove to Blackshear, Ga. for a weekend of Bigfoot research to kick-off this project. Scott and I met up with Kevin and Doris Crawford, and Steve Hester and did a little research where Steve had his sighting. Our time was very limited due to a scheduled meeting that night, so we really didn't have much time to do what we normally would have done, but we did find a few interesting things and accidentally tracked a bear. Below are a few pictures of interesting things we found that we felt were noteworthy because every little piece of the puzzle is important. We try to observe everything, and I must say Scott has an eye for anything out of the ordinary. In just two outings with him, he's already taught me a lot, and it's amazing the things that we as humans ignore and overlook. I will never be able to go into the forest the same ever again.

Just a spot we thought was unique looking, so I took a picture. All the pine straw was pushed away. I later learned that tortoises may do this while mating.

Well, I quickly found out that people in South Georgia don't seem to get in a hurry, and due to a train that is probably still sitting in the same spot, we had to go about 20 miles out of the way and were late for our own meeting. At the restaurant we met up with several locals interested in the topic of Bigfoot, and several shared their stories, which are also included in this report. We had a quiet night of investigation that night, and the unpredicted misty rain for most of the night may have made it quieter than it may have been otherwise. At that point we had to leave Kevin and Doris behind and find a new location on our own. At one point we considered just going back home, even though Scott, John, and April lived over five hours away. We finally decided on a location and began to set up for the night. We had no idea just how crazy and scary our night would soon be.

Because I am such a novice field researcher, literally I am a beginner in the field, I am too scared to sleep in a tent because I like to be able to always see my surroundings. I planned to sleep in my truck, with the keys in the ignition and with my truck aimed to drive straight out just in case something did happen. Scott sleeps in his truck too, but John and April planned to sleep in their tent. They put their tent up at the road line, parked their car beside it, then Scott parked his truck beside them, and on the end was my truck. John had his 4k camera set up on its tripod and Scott had his audio recorder on. We had some smaller thermal scopes, and Scott had his high-powered thermal scope with video recording capabilities. We had a nice little fire going and were sitting around the fire probably 20 feet away from their car. John was sitting with his back towards his car, April was sitting to his left, Scott was sitting directly across from John, and I had my back to the tree line sitting directly between John and Scott. We always try to spread out and watch behind the person in front of us. Anytime someone hears a strange noise, or sees anything unusual, we don't point or draw attention to what we see or hear. We continue to act casual, and say something like, "I just heard a grunt at Scott's 8:00." Pretty sure the ones we encountered this night could care less about us knowing they were there.

It started out very quietly and I was starting to get a little disappointed. I was really wanting to capture some great sounds like the howls we had captured on the last research project I participated in and maybe see something off in the distance. I wanted to see one, but at the same time I didn't. I remember it was about 9:00 p.m. when the coyotes finally started. Scott said, "now the coyotes have started so you can expect things to start happening if they're going to happen." We knew then to get out all our equipment and be ready to scan and record. John got up to check his camera and said, "that's weird, my camera battery is dead, and it's only been going for 10 minutes, and it was fully charged." He replaced that battery with another battery, and it was also dead. It was then I realized maybe my thermal scope also being dead wasn't just a coincidence since I had just charged it and not even used it yet. Scott's thermal scope was also dead, but for some reason his Pulsar Thermal with recording capabilities was not. It was quiet for a little while, and we decided we were going to do some things to hopefully stir up

some activity. We decided to all charge our devices again before we did anything, so hopefully we could capture it. We all had our devices plugged into our vehicles charging, except Scott still had one scope he could still use. No cell phones were affected either.

It was April's first time out and she was scared to death. She threatened several times that she was going to get a motel room, and each time we talked her out of it. I even told her she'd be so proud of herself the next morning. She was very hyper aware of everything. With every sound she'd jump, and she was constantly combing the tree line in front of her, which was behind Scott. I was facing her and watching her, and I could tell that all her senses were on high alert.

Off in the distance we heard an owl, then nothing. After a few minutes April says, "what is that light?" She was pointing at the top of the tree line, but I could not see the light. John then saw it and asked the same question, and that's when he said it looked like an orb. It was weaving through the tops of the trees along the tree line and made the 90 degrees turn to its right to continue following the tree line beside us. It floated to the road and then dropped lower when it reached the road. Once it crossed the road, I was able to see it. What I saw was a white light about the size of a golf ball. It slowly floated directly away from us until it disappeared. I tried very hard to record it with my phone, but because I couldn't see it in the beginning, I wasn't able to, and once I did see it, it was too far away to capture it with a cell phone. I do have the audio of the event as it happened at least, and you can clearly understand what's going on, and what we are seeing during that 2-minute video. It was at this point that Scott said, "well now we know they're here." I think my heart sank a little when he said that.

Things settled down again, and somehow, we still talked April into staying. She was really facing her fears that night, and I was terrified she was going to leave and reduce our numbers. Scott kept telling her she was going to be ok, and they just like to mess with people. He explained they were just watching and curious. April will tell you now, that every time Scott would tell her that, she would hear a voice laughing in her head saying, "are you sure about that?" A few times she did tell us that she felt like she was losing her mind, but we just assumed she was just scared, and all her senses were reacting. John called me the next day and explained the voices she told him she was hearing, and we all agree there's a strong possibility she may have been experiencing what many describe as "mind speak." She eventually told us she felt like they were feeding off her fear. April is very inexperienced in this topic, and she had never even heard of an orb before. For her to be experiencing things and seeing things often reported by others, is just further confirmation that what she was experiencing was real.

It wasn't very long after the orb had faded off, and things settled down a bit, I heard Scott saying, "oh I got you now." I looked and had his thermal pointed in the direction the orb went. He then told us he was looking at one peeking around a tree. He could see both hands on the tree, both knees, and the head peeking. He took several pictures and then switched to record. Once he started recording, he could see that the creature was still squatting down behind the tree, but it had changed position. He recorded for a few minutes and then lost sight of it.

Things settled down again, but only for a short while. John said he heard something cross the dirt road and began having a strong feeling of being watched. He shivered as if his hairs were standing on end and said, "I don't just feel like I'm being watched...I know I am." April heard some things across the road moving around. We heard a strange bird sound but then debunked as an extremely loud cricket close by. The forest was never dead silent like frequently reported. The sounds all seemed normal, except for that one extremely loud cricket. Then April jumped up and said she heard something scratching the back of their tent and that was it for her. She told us that she was getting a motel room. We of course tried to calm her down but there was no chance after she heard something scratching the back of their tent. John decided he'd go with her, and they would come back the next morning to break down the tent and get their belongings.

It was then I heard two growls behind me. I looked over at Scott and he looked at me and said, "that was two growls." That was it for me too. I told John and April to wait on me because I was also leaving. I had no idea where I was going, but I was not staying there. Scott decided those growls were just too close for comfort and we all decided to turn on all our lights, pull the vehicles around with headlights on, and make sure we were all packed so no one would have to come back the next day. Thank God I had brought about five gallons of water and was able to extinguish the fire. When John and April went to breakdown their tent, they discovered that 3 of the straps on the backside that held their fly down had been unhooked. April specifically remembers that after the tent was up, she purposely hooked the straps correctly, so there is no reason all three straps should have become unhooked.

We were just getting everything into our vehicles as fast as possible and trying not to leave any trash. I had everything loaded in my truck. I had thrown a lot of stuff in the back seat and made sure my electronics were all in my front seat. My scope was still in the same spot charging, my phone, flashlight, and purse were all in the front seat and accounted for and that's when I saw it. A large reflecting white ball peeking through the V of a tree. I had looked at the reflective sign that was close-by many times that night because it kept reminding me of a window in the woods, but it was just a sign on one of the trees on the edge of the camping area. This was the first time I had seen two reflections. I have a flashlight that is more of a spotlight, so I reached onto my front seat and grabbed it. I could see clearly all down behind the tree and could find no explanation for the reflection. Scott was close by so I called him over and asked him if he could explain the baseball size reflection, and if it was possibly eyeshine. He said he didn't know and volunteered to walk closer. It was about 40 yards away and Scott was shining his flashlight as well. When Scott was about 20 yards out, he stopped, started backing up, and then turned and hustled to his truck saying, "we need to get out of here NOW." Scott says as he was approaching the reflection, he was able to see both eyes. He saw it blink and drop from about 7-8 feet to about 5-6 feet in

the V of the tree. The creature had walked out of the tree line and was behind the first tree wide enough to hide behind just inside the camping area.

All 3 vehicles sped out of there, and we all met up for a cup of coffee to gather ourselves. John and April decided to get a motel room for the night. I drove 2 ½ hours home, and Scott drove 5 ½ hours home. Scott is a Marine, a seasoned Police Officer, Firearms Instructor, and experienced BFRO investigator, and whatever we encountered that night, made him drive all the way home that night. It wasn't until the next day that I learned Scott had found a tent with an air mattress still inside of it, pulled into the woods when we first arrived as he was scouting the area. It seems that someone before us may have decided to leave in a hurry too. I'm glad I didn't know about the tent in the woods before all of this started, or I may have left with April to get a motel room the minute things got weird.

Disclaimer-I cannot vouch for the accuracy of the eyewitness reports, but each person I spoke with appeared to be of truthful character. They each seemed to be "salt of the earth" people, and I found no reasons to question their credibility.

Scott Deforest checking out a tree break and teaching me things.

Spoiler Alert: We did go back one year later with a larger group and did not see or hear anything. The whole area had been clear cut and there were no hard wood trees. We did not hear a bird or even see a squirrel. My cousin agreed to go on that trip, and he is a die-hard non-believer. I just knew this trip would change his mind, and of course it was dead as a doornail. This is the frustrating part of field research. You usually get nothing when in the field. But oh, when you do... it's life changing.

ten
the conclusion

The following is an excerpt from a previous chapter, but I feel it's worth repeating because it is my best summary to describe how incredible these creatures are. "I can only imagine the super abilities we as humans may have had in the beginning, before we filled our brains and our stomachs with garbage. We allow ourselves to be spoon fed with information and just accept it all as truth. We live in structured environments and have become creatures of habit. We consume the poisons we are fed, to our bodies and our minds. We get up at the same time each morning, travel the same route to work, repeat the same duties each day, travel the same route home, go to bed at the same time each night, and drown ourselves in movies, social media, music, books, etc. These creatures are part of the earth itself. They belong to the night. Deep in the woods, under the cover of darkness is where they thrive. Can you imagine how keen their senses must be? Think of the incredible senses and talents so many animals have, combine all those senses and talents, then add a brain with the ability to think, plan, and communicate. A supernatural force of nature. They remain as organic as the day God made them.

Throughout my adventures in the Bigfoot community, I have been blessed to meet some incredible people, including the late Bob "Grumpy" Wilson. I was only able to share a campfire with him a few times but left an impression on me that will stay with me the remainder of my life. Seeing the impact he made on so many people's lives; it really opened my eyes to just how much like family many of these people become. In his memory and in his honor, Darrell Neese formed a group named S.E.K.R.S. (South-East Kryptid Research Society). This type of group had been a goal of Grumpy's, and I am so appreciative and honored to have received an invitation to join such a spectacular group of people. This group consists of military members, first responders, medical professionals, scientists, a film producer, and many others with reputable and talented backgrounds. This team conducts all types of field investigations, including scientific experiments. I look forward to working with this team and helping capture as much evidence as possible. If there's a team out there that can do it, I truly believe this team can. I have seen some of the results and cannot wait until some are released.

There is so much fascinating information out there just waiting to blow your mind. I encourage you to get to reading. Start looking for information. Search podcasts, read books, watch YouTube videos, and talk to people. If field research interests you, get out there and just make yourself a starting point. You would be amazed at the stories that stay hidden in families for generations. Don't believe everything, but don't discredit everything either. Keep an open mind and think for yourself. I hope you enjoyed reading my little book. It has been a learning experience, and I am sure mistakes were made. I do not claim to be any type of expert, but I do advocate for people in this field who I feel are credible and just want the truth to be revealed., I mean, if you saw something that shouldn't exist, how would you react?

I am already working on my 2nd little book of interesting things that someone with "Bigfoot on the Brain" will hopefully enjoy. See ya soon!

Angie 😊

bibliography

What is a Hominin, Hominid, and a Hominoid? (n.d.). *Amazing*Life.Bio. https://www.amazinglife.bio/biology-course/what-is-a-hominin%2C-horminid%2C-and-a-hominoid%3F

Merritt Herald YouTube. (2024, August 14). *Dr. Jeffrey Meldrum of Idaho States University on relict hominoids-Nicola Valley Bigfoot Conference* [Video]. YouTube. https://www.youtube.com/watch?v=Qww7I1b IONA.

Johnson, A. (2022, February 17). 5 *Amazing Ways Chimps are just like us.* Jane Goodall. https://janegoodall.ca/our-stories/chimp-human-similarities/.

Handwerk, B/ (2021, September 15). An evolutionary timeline of Homo Sapiens. *Smithsonian Magazine.* https://www.smithsonianmag.com/science-nature/essential-timeline-understanding-evolution-homo-sapiens-180976807/.

Biblical Genetics-Patterns of Evidence Foundation (Patterns+). (n.d.). Patterns of Evidence Foundation (Patterns+). https://digitalpatternsofevidence.vhx.tv/biblical-genetics.

Regal B. (2009). Entering dubious realms: Grover Krantz, science, and Sasquatch. Annals of science, 66(1), 83-102. https://doi.org/10.1080/00033790802202421.

M,J. (2024, February 18). Why Were Books Removed out of the Bible? – Josh M – Medium. *Medium.* https://thesevenlamps.medium.com/why-were-books-taken-out-of-the-bible-ec9aad8cflf6.

Bibliography

The Book of Enoch and its importance to anyone interested in biblical history.
(n.d.). https://blog.nes.edu/the_book_of_enoch_and_its_importance_
to_anyone_interested_in_biblical_history.

about the author

Angie Williamson is a Georgia native, and a Bigfoot researcher who officially began her journey into the world of cryptozoology in 2019. Since then, she has immersed herself in all aspects of Bigfoot research, including fieldwork, data analysis of existing research, networking for shared knowledge, and eyewitness interviews.

Angie actively participates in expeditions and field investigations, both privately and as part of a research team. She has a passion for meeting with individuals who claim to have seen Bigfoot or experienced high strangeness in the forest, and she is dedicated to documenting their experiences and bringing these encounter stories to a wider audience.

Angie's eyewitness reports can be found on her Facebook page, "Angie Goes Squatching", and this book marks her debut as an author. Driven by a commitment to uncover the truth about Bigfoot, she is already hard at work on her second book, promising more insights and discoveries.

If you would like to contact the author regarding your encounter story, you may private message her directly on Facebook or through the "Angie Goes Squatching" page. She is always seeking new witnesses.